JOURNAL OF A HESSIAN GRENADIER BATTALION

Translated by
Bruce E. Burgoyne
Edited by
Dr. Marie E. Burgoyne

HERITAGE BOOKS
2008

HERITAGE BOOKS
AN IMPRINT OF HERITAGE BOOKS, INC.

Books, CDs, and more—Worldwide

For our listing of thousands of titles see our website
at
www.HeritageBooks.com

Published 2008 by
HERITAGE BOOKS, INC.
Publishing Division
100 Railroad Ave. #104
Westminster, Maryland 21157

International Standard Book Numbers
Paperbound: 978-0-7884-3157-9
Clothbound: 978-0-7884-7058-5

Other books by Bruce E. Burgoyne:

Eighteenth Century America (A Hessian Report On the People, the Land, the War) As Noted in the Diary of Chaplain Philipp Waldeck (1776-1780)

Enemy Views: The American Revolutionary War as Recorded by the Hessian Participants

Hessian Chaplains: Their Diaries and Duties

Hesse-Hanau Order Books, A Diary and Roster: A Collection of Items Concerning the Hesse-Hanau Contingent of "Hessians" Fighting Against the American Colonists in the Revolutionary War

Most Illustrious Hereditary Prince: Letters to Their Prince from Members of Hesse-Hanau Military Contingent in the Service of England During the American Revolution

A Hessian Officer's Diary of the American Revolution Translated From An Anonymous Ansbach-Bayreuth Diary and The Prechtel Diary

Journal of the Hesse-Cassel Jaeger Corps

Order Book of the Hesse-Cassel von Mirbach Regiment

Hessian Letters and Journals and A Memoir

The Trenton Commanders: Johann Gottlieb Rall and George Washington, as noted in Hessian Diaries

Defeat, Disaster, and Dedication

Revolutionary War Letters Written by Hessian Officers: Generals Wilhelm von Knyphausen, Carl Wilhelm Von Hachenberg, Friedrich Wilhelm von Lossberg, Johann Friedrich Cochenhausen, Friedrich Von Riedesel and Major Carl Leopold von Baurmeister

English Army and Navy Lists, Compiled During the American Revolutionary War by Ansbach-Bayreuth Lieutenant Johann Ernst Prechtel

Journal of the Prince Charles Regiment

The Diary of Lieutenant von Bardeleben and Other von Donop Regiment

Georg Pausch's Journal and Reports of the Campaign in America, as Translated from the German Manuscript in the

Lidgerwood Collection in the Morristown Historical Park Archives, Morristown, N.J.

CD ROMS:
CD: The Hessian Collection, Volume 1: Revolutionary War Era
CD: Ansbach-Bayreuth Diaries from the Revolutionary War
CD: Waldeck Soldiers of The American Revolutionary War
CD: Canada During the America Revolutionary War
CD: A Hessian Report on the People, the Land, the War of Eighteenth Century America, As Noted in the Diary of Chaplain Philipp Waldeck 1776-1780
CD: They Also Served. Women with the Hessian Auxiliaries
CD: A Hessian Diary of the American Revolution
CD: A Hessian Officer's Diary of The American Revolution
CD: Diaries of Two Ansbach Jaegers

Journal
of a
Hessian Grenadier Battalion

Which sailed to America
As the Koehler Grenadier Battalion,
Was later called the Graf Grenadier Battalion,
And finally, the Platte Grenadier Battalion

Translated from a German Language copy
In the Lidgerwood Collection
in the Morristown National Historical Park
Morristown, NJ

By
Bruce E. Burgoyne
And Edited by
Dr. Marie E. Burgoyne

Introduction

When England found it necessary to hire troops to serve in America, Colonel William Faucitt was sent to a number of German courts to negotiate treaties to hire those troops. Eventually six states, Hesse-Cassel, Hesse-Hanau, Brunswick, Waldeck, Ansbach-Bayreuth, and Anhalt-Zerbst, furnished units which traveled to America. By far the largest contingent was provided by Hesse-Cassel, and all the troops were commonly called Hessians.

The units from Hesse-Cassel included sixteen infantry regiments, four grenadier battalions, eventually a corps of jaegers, some artillery, and a large hospital staff. Those units served in America from 1776 to 1783, and some units did not return to Germany until 1784. One of the grenadier battalions was the Koehler Grenadier Battalion, which, following several name changes, became the Platte Grenadier Battalion. As a general rule, the unit name changed whenever the commander changed.

The following translation was made from a copy of the Platte Grenadier Battalion Journal in the Lidgerwood Collection at the Morristown National Historical Park in Morristown, New Jersey. As was the custom with most Hessian units serving England during the American Revolutionary War, the journal was maintained by the battalion quartermaster, in this case Karl Bauer.

In making my translation, the work was simplified by occasional references to a translation by a Miss Raahage, in England, possibly in the mid-1930's. I know nothing more about her. Her translation seems to have been done very quickly, and typed as she translated, as many errors, repeat phrasing, and strike-overs would seem to indicate. However, it did enable me to more quickly make my translation. As always, I must caution persons using the translation for research purposes to use the translation as a quick reference, but to verify the content by returning to the original document.

I have taken certain liberties in making my translation. The dates are as entered in the German language text, but I have used an e after the vowels a, o, and u, when necessary to indicate an umlaut. I have also inserted additional identifying information on individuals, whenever possible, using Inge Auerbach and Otto Froehlich's *Hessische Truppen im Amerikanischen Unabhaengigkeitskrieg, (Hetrina)*, 5 vols., (Marburg, 1972-76), as the source for most Hessian names. Spelling of names of persons and places have been changed to the current, or more generally accepted form in some cases. When a person or place could not be further identified, I have used the author's spelling as given in the German text.

Parenthesis in the translation are as used by the

author, and my additions and notations are within brackets. The charts are from the Raahage translation. A few notes have been added, in brackets, primarily for the information of the general reader, not familiar with some of the terms used in the journal. Finally, I must apologize for inconsistencies in the use of capital letters when writing about men and units. I have tried to use capitals only when referring to specific units.

Bruce E. Burgoyne
Dover, DE

Journal

1776

On the 14th, 15th, and 16th of February, in accordance with orders, the four flank companies of the Rall, Stein, Wissenbach, and Buenau Regiments marched out of their respective quarters and into cantonment quarters in Wolfhagen. There they were formed into a grenadier battalion, the command of which was entrusted to Lieutenant Colonel [Johann Christoph von] Koehler, and received his name.

The company commanders and officers of the battalion were:

1) Captain [Friedrich Wilhelm] Bode, 1st Lieutenant [August Friedrich von] Linckersdorf, 2nd Lieutenants [Johann Christoph] Muehlhausen and [Wilhelm] Studenroth, from the company of the Stein Regiment.

2) Captain [Johannes] Neumann, Staff Captain [Johann Wilhelm] Bode, 1st Lieutenant [Christoph Ludwig] von Romrodt, and 2nd Lieutenant [Andreas] Oelhans, from the company of the Stein Regiment.

3) Captain [Georg] Hohenstein [1st] Lieutenant [Friedrich Wilhelm] Huepeden, [1st] Lieutenant [Johann Anton] von Dalwigk, and [2nd] Lieutenant [Wilhelm] Stippich, from the company of the

Wissenbach Regiment.

4) Captain [Henrich Christian] Hessenmueller, [1st] Lieutenant [Johann Jakob] Fritsch, and [2nd] Lieutenants [Balthasar] Mertz and [Johann Henrich] Brauns, from the company of the Buenau Regiment.

The non-commissioned officers were taken mostly from other field regiments, and the privates were nearly all raw recruits called up for the first time.

From the sixteenth to the end of the month, the troops were issued uniforms and weapons. They were drilled twice a day. As it was still very cold, this was done in small groups in houses and barns, and, weather permitting, outdoors.

When the weather began to improve, during the first days of March, the battalion conducted training in the fields outside the city.

On 5 March, Lieutenant Muehlhausen was transferred to the Rall Regiment, and [2nd] Lieutenant [Karl] von Dalwigk, Jr., replaced him.

Otherwise, nothing occurred during the month except for a continuation of training. Everyone prepared for the anticipated departure. Constant turnovers were made of the untrainable for men who could be trained. This situation made the work of the officers even more difficult, because the new replacements were nothing but raw farm boys, which greatly hindered the completion of training.

All the various uniforms and weapons which the companies had brought from their previous regiments were delivered to the local commissary at Spangenberg, and as of now the battalion has been outfitted with the same new equipment.

On 19 and 20 March, the battalion fired live ammunition for the first time.

We remained peacefully in our cantonment quarters throughout the month of April. Training continued as in the previous month, and the weather was very pleasant.

The 4th of May - At one o'clock in the night we received orders by special messenger for our departure along the following march route: On 6 May the Koehler Grenadier Battalion is to march from Wolfhagen. The staff and one company are to go to Obervellmar, one company to Heckershausen, one and one-half companies to Niedervellmar, and a half company to Frommershausen, in the District of Kassel. On 5 May the quartermaster sergeants and their guard forces are to set out to arrange for quarters in the above listed villages.

This evening, however, a change in marching orders arrived at the battalion, which changed the departure until the eighth, and changed the march route. On 8 May the Grenadier Battalion Koehler is to march from Wolfhagen to Hofgeismar. On 9 May the staff and two companies are to go to Bodenfelde, and two companies to Wahnbeck, in the District of Hannover, in [the territory of] Hannover, crossing the Weser River at Gieselwerder. 10 May is to be a day of rest.

The quartermaster sergeants and their guard forces also received a change of orders. They are to leave Obervellmar tomorrow morning and go to Hofgeismar, where they are to arrange for quarters.

According to the orders, the seriously ill and the baggage are to be taken to Kassel tomorrow, where everything is to be put on boats and sent to Bremen. The battalion received ten wagons for transporting the remaining baggage and the less seriously ill on the march.

The 8th of May - Early this morning the battalion marched from Wolfhagen toward Hofgeismar, with a full complement, except for one man short from Captain Bode's Company.

The 9th of May - The battalion marched from

Hofgeismar, crossed the Weser River at Gieselwerder, and arrived in quarters at Bodenfelde and Wahnbeck, according to the above noted orders.

The 10th of May - At both of the previously noted places we had a day of rest, and today received the march route [see the chart on the following page] from Major General [Martin] Schmidt, with the order that the battalion has been assigned to his brigade. The quarters in the villages were good, and the troops were well-fed.

The vacancy in Captain Bode's Company was filled here so that the battalion is at full strength.

The 11th of May - The battalion marched to the previously designated quarters at Vahle, Bellensen, Dinckelshausen, Volpriehausen, and Grieswald.

The 12th - The battalion marched to Olendorf, Hilvershausen, Dietersen, Eilensen, Ellensen, and Krimmansen, in the District of Hundsdrueck.

We received strict orders from General [Wilhelm] von Knyphausen that the best discipline be maintained and that the troops should demand nothing while in quarters except that which their hosts voluntarily provided.

A better order was to be maintained with the

baggage wagons. As of today the provisioning of the non-commissioned officers and the privates by the hosts was to be without charge. The quarters and rations were terrible and many individuals complained that they were not provided with the least bit.

The 13th - Today was a day of rest.

The 14th - The battalion marched to the previously designated quarters, which were occupied as follows: the staff and Captain Bode's Company at Eime, Neumann's Company at Meinholte and Vorholte, Hohenstein's Company at Wangestadt, and Captain Hessenmueller's Company at Linne and Linnecamp.

The quarters and rations were as on the twelfth. In most of the houses not even straw [to sleep on] was provided.

The 15th - The battalion entered the assigned quarters at Esperde and Brockensen, which were no better than the previous ones.

The 16th - We marched across the battlefield near Hastenbeck, which village we passed. The quarters which we entered today at Grosshilligsfeld and Kleinhilligsfeld, at Rohrsen and Offersen were better than those previously occupied. The noted villages lie about three and three-quarters miles from Hameln. [These appear to be German miles, or about 20

1st Division 1st Brigade			March route for the Kohler Grenadier Battn from the 10th to the 17th May incl. 1776											
Quarters in Hesse on the 10th May 1776	To march the 11th May 1776	Companies	The 12th	Companies	The 13th	Companies	The 14th	Companies	The 15th	Companies	16th	Companies	The 17th
Bodenfeld and Wahnbeck in Hanover.	Vahle Staff Bellensen Dunkle=hausen Volprechhausen & Grünewald	1 1 1 1	Ohlendorf. Staff & Hilwers=hausen. Dietersen Eilersen in Hundes=ruck.	1 1 1	Rest day		Einie. Staff and Meinhotte Vorwolle Lenne Wanglen=stadt Linnecamps in Wickensen in Brunswick	1 1 2/3 1 1/3	Esperde. Staff and Brockensen in Grohnte in Brunswick	2½ 1½	Gross & Klein=hillings=feld. Staff & Rohersen Afferesen in Springe	2 1 1	Rest day
The quarters for Maj. Gen Schmidt are in Lippelsberg	in Uslar		At Dassella		Restday		The town of Asshershausen		Hajen in Grohunde		Hachmullen in Springe		Restday

English miles.]

The 17th - A day of rest.

The 18th - From the previously noted quarters to Lauenau, Feggendorf, and Pohle, occupied by the staff and Captain Bode's Company, Messencamp and Altenhagen by Captain Hessenmueller's Company, Huelsede, Meinsen, and Schmarye by half of Captain Hohenstein's Company and half of Neumann's [sic].

These were rather good quarters in appearance, as was the provisioning for non-commissioned officers and privates.

The 19th - We marched past Rodenburg [in the territory of] Schaumburg and into the following quarters: the staff, Bode's and Neumann's Companies at Gross Munzel, Hessenmueller's Company at Oster Munzel, and Hohenstein's Company at Holtensen.

These are the best quarters that we have yet had. The staff of the Estdorff Cavalry Regiment is at Gross Munzel. There is a beautiful riding school here for the use of the cavalry. Horse breeding appears to be successful, so there are many rich horse merchants living in this village. The District of Blumenau, in which the mentioned villages are located, appears to be in better circumstances than the others that we have passed.

Another order, a repetition of the previous one, was received from Lieutenant General von Knyphausen, that the best discipline and conduct must be maintained by the officers, non-commissioned officers, and privates.

The 20th - From the above quarters we marched to the following quarters, passing Neustadt on the Ruebenberge *en route* in the Vogter Mandelslohe, in the District of Neustadt on the Ruebenberge. Beyond Neustadt the great heath began. Today's march was through a dismal region, the most severe that we have yet encountered. Today we passed the Cloister of Mariensee.

The quarters in Madelslohe Mandelsdorf in the Wicke, and Amedorf, were quite good. The region between the Mariensee and Mandelslohe was also rather fertile.

The 21st - A day of rest.

The 22nd - Through the city of Rethem and into the following quarters: the staff and Captain Bode's Company to Wohlendorf, Hedern, and Donnershorst, Captain Neumann's Company to Stoecken, Captain Hohenstein's and Captain Hessenmueller's Companies to Huelsen, in the District of Rethem. The quarters of the non-commissioned officers and privates were so-

so in part, and in part absolutely worthless.

The 23rd - We crossed the Aller River and entered quarters at Verden. In addition to our regiment, the Huyn Regiment was also quartered here.

The 24th of May - We crossed the Wuemme, a small river of no importance, and the staff and Captain Bode's Company went to Ahausen, Captain Hohenstein's Company to Eversen, Captain Hessenmueller's Company to Imterstedt, and Captain Neumann's Company to Hellwege, in the District of Rotenburg.

Although today's march was through a depressing region and across a great heath, where nothing but goats and sheep were to be seen, the quarters were even more pitiful. Also, everyone expected the charges for the non-commissioned officers' and privates' rations to be demanded even more strongly. Officially there would be no question as to how many men were actually fed, but only how many billets had been used.

The 25th - A day of rest.

The 26th - The battalion marched into the following quarters: the staff and one-half of Captain Bode's Company to Kirchtimke, one and one-half companies, Captain Neumann's and half of Captain Bode'a to Bredorf, one company, Captain

Hohenstein's, to Westertimke, and one company, Captain Hessenueller's, to Neuen Buelstedt .

In all these villages the quarters were like the previous ones, and in such a rough region nothing better could be expected. Three officials and two foresters made it absolutely clear that the rations were to be properly charged, even if they did not know how many had actually been delivered, and despite having been told that many of the troops, who were provided with quarters, received nothing.

The 27th - The battalion continued to march through a dreary region, where nothing but heath and sand were to be seen, and into quarters.

The staff and Captain Bode's Company went to Selsingen, Captain Neumann's Company to Haasel and Parnewinkel, Captain Hohenstein's Company to Deinstedt and Ochtenhausen, and Captain Hessemueller's Company to Graanstadt in the District of Zeven.

The quarters were so-so. Selsingen is a rather pleasant place. Here for the first time the officials put us under the regulations of the Hannover government regarding rations and the wagon and saddle horses. The natives were to be paid for these items. Here, also, we learned that each man's rations were to paid for at the rate of two groschen per day. The officials and their assistants had never previously made the least mention of this part of their instructions, intentionally, in so far as possible, no doubt, as disputes might otherwise arise regarding the receipt of rations issued but not delivered to the men.

The 28th of May - Today we passed Bremervoerde, a rather pretty, well laid-out little city, lying to the east [of Bremen]. Here, it was already possible to see the Elbe River and to notice the tide. We marched out of Selsingen this morning at daybreak, and during the late asfternoon arrived in Koehler and Ringstaedt. The staff and companies of Captain Bode and Hessenmueller were in the first, and the companies of Captain Neumann and Hohenstein in the latter. Most of yesterday's march was made in sand and heath. The region of both of the above villages was wretched, which could also be said of the quarters. Here we received orders so that we could be prepared for the muster which is about to take place, and the embarkation which is to follow. Six hundred dollars are to be paid in advance for the necessary provisions for the officers for the month of June. At the same time, we were notified that upon entering cantonment quarters the rations, which the non-commissioned officers and privates had received at no cost to this time, would cease.

The 29th of May - This was a day of rest.

The 30th of May - The battalion entered cantonment quarters. The staff and the companies of Captains Bode, Hohenstein, and Hessenmueller were in the parish of Dorum, Captain Neumann's Company in the parish of Misselwarden.

The region around was pleasant and very fertile. The inhabitants are friendlier than those we met in other places on our march, despite our having to give credit to the Hannoverians for having shown every consideration in their power. Nevertheless, we must praise our present cantonment quarters even more. They took a pleasure in serving us, which was especially welcome in view of our pending embarkation, and the need for adequate provisions.

The 2nd of June - This morning we received orders to take leave of our good hosts and to march to Ritzebuettel.

The 3rd of June - We moved out from our cantonment quarters at six o'clock this morning, and entered Ritzebuettel toward ten o'clock. The many people who accompanied us, part on horseback, part on foot, were innumerable. As it was very warm, and the road from Dorum to Ritzebuettel is very sandy, our escort made the march quite unpleasant for us. Because of the great amount of dust it was nearly impossible to see one step ahead. Many of them expressed their sympathy, but could not understand the sweat on our overheated brows. Ritzebuettel is a village built primarily along a single street, and it has no resemblance to a city. The houses are built in a Dutch style, mostly small, but quite attractive. On one of the small islands lying in the Elbe, reached by a bridge, the Huyn Regiment was mustered upon our arrival, and immediately taken into service and embarked. As soon as the Huyn Regiment left the spot, our regiment marched in and then followed the Huyn Regiment. The Seitz Regiment followed the Koehler Grenadier Battalion. Captain [Johann] Ewald's Jaeger Company had been mustered, taken the oath, and been embarked before the Huyn Regiment. This company of jaegers, our staff and Captain Bode's and Captain Hessenmueller's Companies of the Koehler Grenadier Battalion were embarked on the transport ship *De Riviere Divina*, Captain Neumann's and Captain Hohenstein's

Companies on the *Vrou Classina.* The latter was a Dutch ship from Hamburg.

The 4th of June - The heavy baggage and campaign necessities arrived at Ritzebuettel from Kassel and were loaded aboard ship.

The 5th of June - The Wissenbach Regiment was embarked.

Although our ship was the largest in the fleet, there were too many men on board, and all of them could not find a berthing space. The heat between decks is exceedingly great. If, as promised by Colonel [William] Faucitt, some of the men are not transferred to another ship when we reach Portsmouth, it is to be feared that a contagious disease will strike us. The officers and non-commissioned officers and privates aboard the *Vrou Classina* have more comfortable conditions, and are not as crowded together as on our ship. A second unpleasant situation on board our ship, which I have noticed, is that the provisions are not nearly as good as on the mentioned ship. They receive food items which we do not get.

In addition to the other three companies noted, we have the artillery detachment with us. In the cabin, which is small in proportion to the ship, there are fifteen people. The cleanliness aboard our ship can not be compared with that on the *Vrou Classina*, and therefore it is obvious that our ship's captain is not a Hollander.

The captain has nothing to say about the provisions, as that, on all non-English ships of the fleet, is under the direction of an Englishman called the superintendent, who is supposedly a midshipman from a warship.

The provisioning was done in Hamburg and it is the agent's fault that it is so bad, because, according to rumor, he has made a profit on it. Zwieback, made from coarse rye grain, has been delivered instead of wheat flour, as on other ships. The water already stinks. This is the result of buying old wine barrels in which red wine has been, rather than new, or even old, water kegs. The individual negotiating the purchase should have known better, at least that is what our superintendent assured us. The ship, counting the captain and mates, of which there are three, has a crew of 45 sailors. It is already rather old, and was built on the Divina River in Russia, hence the name. It is 140 feet long and 33 feet wide. Most of us had relied upon the ship's rations, and therefore had seldom taken into account the purchase of rations. Now, many are sadder but wiser. Some had been prevented from buying fresh provisions due to economic circumstances, and others, who did not face this situation, were unable to obtain much, even for hard cash. All the things which we have learned are necessary for our pending voyage are simple articles, the purchase of which no one gave any thought while still in Ritzebuettel. It was clear that few ships departed this harbor supplied with these same articles. Another reason we were so ill prepared was because no one knew what to take on such a voyage. Those of us who had previously been to sea did not know, and could even less advise others. We had to wait patiently until we reached England.

The 7th of June - We lay at anchor.

The 8th of June - The remaining troops and horses were embarked.

The 9th of June - At a quarter after four this morning, the agent fired a cannon shot and raised a flag as a signal for the fleet to depart. An hour later the entire fleet sailed out. It consisted of nineteen large transport ships. Upon our departure, a Hamburg yacht, which lay in the harbor, and which had twelve metal 4-pounders on board, saluted us. This yacht was very beautiful, well-built, and decorated. It belonged to a native of Hamburg, who has been appointed a magistrate in Ritzebuettel. We were also saluted by the cannon on land. The cannons on the ship, although few, answered the salute. Toward eleven o'clock, midday, we entered the open sea, which was indicated by a red barrel buoy. To our left, at a distance, we could see several ships stranded during the past fall and winter. A number of people appeared to be exercising their right to salvage. During the onset of night, we passed near Helgoland, off to the north. As a warning to ships in this region, a lighthouse could be seen on a height. We saw very many seals here. The sea was calm, which made the first day of our journey all the more pleasant. The wind was east-southeast, and we traveled ten [English] miles in an hour.

The 10th of June - The sea was restless and the journey not as pleasant as yesterday. Today we sailed six miles an hour with a southwest wind.

The 11th of June - The sea was very rough. At nine o'clock in the evening we had a very strong storm. Seasickness took hold among us today and everyone wished to be back in our Fatherland. The wind was south to east and we covered fifteen miles today. [There is no certain way to know when the author used German miles, and when he used English miles. One German mile is equal to six English miles.]

The 12th of June - The voyage was rather peaceful again today, and we traveled as far as yesterday.

Although there was a wind calm for a while, we sailed twelve miles with a wind from the south to east. We sailed from 54° 50' north latitude and at noon today at 53°19' north latitude according to sun sightings. This evening we passed Texel, at a great distance to the southwest.

The 13th of June - The wind was rather variable from the northwest to west by north. We sailed only eight miles, and were at 53° north latitude. Toward eight o'clock in the evening a heavy fog set in, so that none of the other ships could be seen. Everything on the ship had a white covering as in late fall.

The 14th of June - Because of a continuous south-southwest wind we had to tack today, but still sailed nine miles. We were at 52°20' north latitude at noon today, according to the sun sighting. The weather was very cold.

The 15th - The southwest wind swung to the south. It was rather cool and we sailed nine miles. As the weather was very dull, we could not take a noon sighting today.

The 16th of June - We had rather stormy weather. A grenadier named Lohmann, of Captain Bode's Company, died early this morning of a high fever. He was left lying until this evening. I ask the reason and the ship's captain told me that he did not like to throw a body overboard during the day. During the evening the body was sewn in a hammock and blanket, in which stones and sand had been placed. It was the full cost of the burial, if I do not include a bottle of cognac, which Captain Bode gave the sailors for their efforts.

We had rainy weather all day, but it was so light at noon that we could take a sun sight. Accordingly, we were at 51°37' north latitude. We sailed only five miles today.

The 17th of June - The sea was still very stormy, and we sailed seven miles with a contrary west-northwest wind.

The 18th of June - At sunrise, to our great joy, we saw the English and French coasts. Because it was so near, everything on the English coast was clearly distinguishable. As we drew nearer to Dover, however, we could clearly see everything in the region of Calais. We could not see Calais itself, although we tacked in the English Channel with a northwest wind during the afternoon and advanced no more than nine miles. According to the noon sighting, we were at 51°11' north latitude.

The 19th of June - With a weak southeast wind, we

sailed in the Channel, close to the English coast. The bright and beautiful weather was most pleasant today. It was possible to see the fertile fields, beautiful cities, villages, and estates, constantly changing and distinctly separate from one another, along the English coast. The pleasure which existed on every ship in the fleet, and which could be discerned by the pleasant shouts of jubilation, emphasized the day's enjoyment, and caused many to retire to their beds this evening happier than they would be upon arising tomorrow morning.

The 20th of June - We sailed today with a moderate east wind, past the counties of Sussex and Northampton. Toward four o'clock in the afternoon, we reached the Isle of Wight. Toward seven o'clock in the evening we passed the red barrel buoy, and dropped anchor at eleven o'clock at night near Spithead. The betting as to the arrival time in the harbor was to be determined by when the music began, which was also agreed upon by those not betting and who financed their enjoyment from their own money. This closed the day even more happy and carefree than yesterday. We had sailed 24 miles to get here from Dover, and 114 miles from Ritzebuettel. Anyone can see that the miles had not been traveled in a straight line from Ritzebuettel to Portsmouth, otherwise we would have sailed far beyond the latter place.

The 21st of June - Although everyone had gone to bed rather late yesterday evening, at sunrise everyone was up on deck. Behind us we could see the fertile and beautiful Isle of Wight, before us Portsmouth, and all around us a great number of warships and transport ships. The *Barfleur,* 98 cannons, was the largest ship in the harbor and more impressive than the others

The warships, for the most part, were something new for us to see and held most of our attention because we had none in our fleet from Ritzebuettel, but were only under the command of Lieutenant Hill of the navy, who acted as the agent. He had sailed on the transport ship *Duke William* with Lieutenant General von Knyphausen. The transport ships lying here were loaded in part with English, the 2nd Division of Brunswickers, a company of Hesse-Hanau artillery, and a regiment of Waldeckers. All these were bound for North America with us.

Today Captain [Charles] Fielding, of the frigate *Ambuscade,* 32 cannons, took over command of the fleet. Lieutenants [Johann Friedrich Jakob] Treutwetter, [Friedrich Wilhelm] von Grothausen, and [Gottlieb Adam] Hofgarten, of Captain Ewald's Company of Jaegers went into Portsmouth today. The latter did not return, and as the others could give no explanation for his absence, we were greatly distressed.

The 22nd - We received our first pay in guineas and bank notes. Upon landing, Lieutenant General von Knyphausen was honored [by the citizens of] Portsmouth with the ringing of bells. Portsmouth is a medium size, but not regularly laid out city. It appears to have a good harbor with extensive trade and to be well fortified. The forwardness of the females of a certain class, and the openness with which they openly invited us into their houses, seemed rather strange to us. Some of the gentlemen were not prevented by the language barrier from accepting the friendly invitations. They will be fortunate to return aboard the ship as healthy as when they left it. Gosport lies opposite Portsmouth to the west. A small arm of the sea separates them from one another. A hospital lying on the shore ahead of our ship presents a fine view.

The 23rd of June - The sea was rather restless. Yesterday a great many small boats with foodstuffs and other items for sale, sailed among the fleet, but today there is not a single one to be seen. When we asked the reason for this, we received as an answer that it was Sunday. Some of those from our ship found this so prevalent in Portsmouth that they could obtain nothing to eat, and therefore had to return aboard ship.

The 24th of June - We remained at anchor. The sea was rather rough.

The 25th of June - The Jaeger Company was transferred from our ship and went aboard another transport ship.

The 26th - We remained lying at anchor.

The 27th of June - Many of the ships lying about us raised anchor and moved to St. Helens, including the Brunswickers and the Hanau Artillery, which moved there and anchored. Reportedly, these ships will not sail with us, but will travel by another route.

The 28th of June - At seven o'clock in the evening we weighed anchor and joined the ships, which had moved out yesterday, at the heights. As soon as the entire fleet had assembled, the commodore fired a shot for our departure. All the ships instantly raised anchor, and with a northwest wind, set sail for North America.

The 29th of June - We could no longer see the English coast. With a northwest wind, we cruised leisurely along the coast near Portsmouth.

The 30th of June - We sailed along peacefully with a very weak northwest wind and slowly entered the English Channel. At five o'clock in the evening the wind again became contrary and we again approached very near the English coast. We could see it very clearly as we went within three miles, in the region of

Plymouth.

The 1st of July - The sea was very rough and we proceeded very slowly with a contrary northwest wind.

The 2nd of July - We tacked near Plymouth with a northwest wind, because our ship, bound for the Western Hemisphere, could not get out of the Channel against a contrary wind. We busied ourselves today fishing for mackerel, which have a good flavor but are not very big, and seldom weigh more than a pound.

The 3rd of July - We spent the day like yesterday, but the catch was greater. The wind from the west-northwest.

The 4th of July - The wind changed this afternoon, more in our favor, and we drew three or four miles closer to Falmouth.

The 5th of July - Early this morning we caught sight of the most fertile and pleasant fields surrounding Falmouth. Not long thereafter the wind became contrary, to our great sorrow. Toward five o'clock in the afternoon we had to turn about, and sailed back toward Plymouth. During the night, a northwest to west wind made us very uncomfortable. One of the largest transport ships, called *Margaretha Elisabetha*, from Hamburg, on which were Colonel [Franz Karl

Erdmann] von Seitz, as well as 480 men of the Stein Regiment and nineteen officers, lost the mainmast during the night.

The 6th of July - The continuous stormy weather and the contrary southwest wind made it necessary to seek shelter in the harbor at Plymouth. At eight o'clock in the morning, the commodore signaled for us to enter. The fleet immediately changed course and steered for the designated harbor. At ten o'clock in the morning we passed a lighthouse called Eddystone, standing on a small rock in the middle of the sea. We had passed this tower, lying to our north, three days ago. It is about three miles from Plymouth. From Portsmouth to this tower, we had traveled 38 miles. At three o'clock in the afternoon we dropped anchor near Plymouth. As the harbor runs very far inland, and is narrow, the entrance conditions were very difficult without a favorable wind. The land on both sides is very high and rocky. The smallest ships from our fleet went very close to the city. The larger ones, however, had to remain at a distance of about five miles from it.

The 7th of July - We still lie here.

The 8th of July - We visited Plymouth. It is a small city, irregularly laid out, lying on a small hill, but heavily populated. For the defense of the harbor, it had several not very strong forts. However, because these are only on the water side and directed against a landing, and enemy ships must first approach rather close to the land before they can attack these forts, and because they are aligned quite parallel to the water, a ship would be at great risk in attacking them, and be even more so considering that the forts would be supported by warships in the harbor.

Our superintendent escorted us aboard the *Foudryant,* 80 cannons, at the docks, which had been captured from the French in the last war. The great magnificence, and comfort of this ship arouse our wonder. The politeness with which the officers on board received us, made us very grateful. From this ship we went to the dock, where many new ships were being built, and all the old ones repaired in the dry dock. The dockyard is an open area, similar to a small settlement. The streets are wide and straight. It is more beautiful than Plymouth, and lies about an English mile from that city. To the southwest of our fleet lay a splendid estate called Edgecomb. Its garden and parks were laid out beautifully in the English manner. In the first, we encountered a great many deer. The house lay at the foot of a high hill, near the water. The hill rose to a considerable height, on which were located a church and a cemetery. From the church, across the harbor, there was as splendid a view of Plymouth, the dock, and in the distance, England, as far as the eye could see; toward the south and east, the Channel.

The 12th of July - We were busy today taking aboard provisions to replace those already used. To save the salted provisions, fresh meat was delivered on some days, as had happened at Portsmouth. At noon today the wind changed so that we could depart. The admiral, or more correctly, the commodore, at once gave the signal to raise the anchor. Before this could take place, the wind again swung to our disadvantage, and we had to remain at anchor.

The 19th of July - At seven o'clock this evening a signal was given for the fleet to depart. However, we had to remain at anchor until seven o'clock in the morning on the twentieth, until the ships surrounding us had sailed out. Nevertheless, as we had to take aboard beer and water this morning, we could not raise the anchor before ten o'clock. We arrived at the lighthouse at one o'clock in the afternoon, but as soon as the fleet entered the Channel, the wind veered again to the northwest.

The 21st of July - It was very stormy during the night and we were driven back to the region of Portsmouth by a southwest to west and a west wind.

The 22nd of July - We sailed to the region of the

province of Cornwall. Because of contrary west to west [sic] winds and west winds we had to lay to at evening near the tip of land at Goodstadt.

The 23rd - The wind was south-southwest. From yesterday until noon today we advanced four miles.

The 24th of July - With clear, bright weather, the wind came from the west-southwest.

The 25th - We reached the vicinity of Falmouth, but here we again had to turn about. The weather was exceptionally pleasant, the wind southwest to south, and according to the noon sighting we were at 49°50' north latitude.

The 26th - We reached the outermost point of England, called Land's End, but could no longer see it. The weather was as yesterday. Because of continuous contrary wind calm, we sailed no distance today. This induced me, Captain Bode, and Lieutenant Linckersdorf to write letters to Hesse. We put them in a well-corked bottle, and threw them into the ocean. However, our courier took just the opposite direction from that which we desired, and went out to sea. Sunset this evening, which appeared as a fire-like pyramid, gradually sinking into the sea, presented us with the most magnificent display in the world.

The 27th of July - About two o'clock this

afternoon, accompanied by rather stormy weather and a northwest wind, we entered the Bay of Biscay. We had now left the English coast, and with it, the land of Europe.

The 28th of July - We sailed ten miles with a weak northwest wind.

The 29th of July - It was cold and unpleasant. Today we were at 48°14' north latitude. The wind was from the west and we sailed fourteen miles.

The 30th of July - There was a thick fog all day. The wind was northeast and supposedly we have sailed nine miles.

The 31st of July - A northeast wind drove us 23 miles. Other ships which could not sail as well, however, forced us to tack. It was rather warm.

The 1st of August - Today, to our great disappointment, we had contrary south-southeast and south winds. The weather was unpleasant and foggy. Many sharks of an unimaginable large size were seen blowing water into the air. According to the noon sighting we were at 47°21' north latitude.

The 2nd of August - We had very pleasant weather. The wind from the northwest, drove us ten miles.

The 3rd of August - The weather was very warm and the wind favorable, but very weak, almost a calm. Last night we sailed eleven miles with a north wind.

A grenadier named Steinmetz, of Captain Hessen-mueller's Company, who died last night, was buried before daybreak. When we think back that we have been aboard ship for two months and have covered only such a short part of our voyage, and that our provisions grow worse as we go further south - especially the salted meat and beer smell bad and turn sour - everyone grows more melancholy. This is increased by the comments of the ship's crew that we can not hope for better winds before the end of this month.

The 4th of August - The wind was variable from the north, and we sailed eleven miles with it. We were supposedly at 46°45' north latitude.

The 5th of August - With a strong north wind and high seas, we sailed twenty miles today. According to the noon sighting, we were at 46°09' north latitude.

The 6th of August - Today we had a rather strong wind, from north to east. The waves were very high. The latitude was 45°43', and we sailed twenty miles today.

The 7th of August - In very stormy weather, and with a northeast wind, we sailed seventeen and one-half miles.

The 8th of August - Our voyage was more peaceful than yesterday. We sailed twenty miles with a northwest wind. It was noticeable that the days are not as long as they are in more northern latitudes at this time of year. We went steadily more southward.

The 9th of August - We sailed eighteen miles in alternating rain and sunshine.

The 10th of August - Today we saw a very large fish, at a distance from the fleet. Also, some turtles swam past our ship. With a west wind, we sailed nineteen miles. We went more to the south than to the west, thus making little headway. The weather was very stormy.

The 11th of August - The stormy weather abated. It was very bright and pleasant. Also, the wind from the south was more favorable for us than yesterday. We sailed 21 and ¼ miles today.

The 12th of August - We again had a contrary west wind with which we sailed seventeen miles, but generally steered a southerly course.

The 13th of August - We encountered an exceptional heat. The wind was from the northwest and drove us toward the south. According to today's sighting we were at 38°04' north latitude, and had sailed twelve miles.

The 14th of August - With a southwest wind, we had raw and unpleasant weather. While turning the ship, we were nearly run down by a ship loaded with provisions. We were in the greatest peril, but it passed without any harm. According to the noon observation. we were at 37°16' north latitude. This led us to believe that we were bound, not for the northern, but for the southern provinces of North America. If we were going to Halifax, in Nova Scotia, we had already steered ten degrees too far to the south.

The 15th of August - At nine o'clock this morning, during a wind calm, a horse ship of the 17th English Dragoon Regiment collided with our ship. It was a Dutch ship, the *Rogge Bloem*, and much larger than ours. It hit in the middle of our ship and the bowsprit caught in our sails and rigging, tearing away not only some sails and rigging, but also the bowsprit. The alarm on board ship was general, and each faced the danger which created the alarm, but could not think of a means of saving himself. If it were stormy or windy, it is possible the ship could have sunk before anyone thought of averting the danger. However, the damage suffered was only to the sails and rigging, and the loss of some ropes and the bowsprit. We were at 37°22' north latitude and had sailed five miles.

The 16th of August - The wind was from the northeast and southeast, and we were in the same latitude as yesterday.

The 17th of August - We had beautiful, warm weather with a contrary southwest wind.

The 18th of August - The weather was stormy with an unpleasant rain.

The 19th of August - During the morning we saw the island of St. Michael ahead of us, to the south. We passed it lying about four German miles to the south. At sunset we discovered the tip of a mountain toward the west, on the island of St. George. We passed it at a distance of about nine miles. Due to the onset of darkness, it was soon lost from sight. Both belong to the Western [Azores] Islands, and we were not a little bit disturbed at having seen them, as thereby we were made aware that we had not yet completed half of our voyage. Our concern was increased when we considered the provisions which we received were worse every day, and that which we had purchased had become scarce. The water grew worse from day to day, and several barrels of salted meat had already been condemned. The individuals in the cabin went to bed this evening in a rather melancholy mood after considering these things.

The 20th of August - We passed the island of Terceira, lying to the north. We were also aware of land lying to our south. Our mate said it was the western part of St. Michael. Supposedly, we were at 38° today. At twelve o'clock there was such a heavy fog that we could not observe the height of the sun, and the islands were lost from view. The two islands lie about ten miles apart and we sailed between them.

The 21st of August - This morning we saw the island of Pico to the north. A high mountain of the same name rises in the form of a sugar loaf above the clouds, which completely covered the island below. This made a majestic view. The island is about ten German miles in length. The Azores Islands produce mainly wine, fruit, and garden produce. Today a grenadier of Captain Hessenmueller's Company died.

The 22nd of August - It has never rained as hard, previously, as it did today. During the afternoon there was a sudden change to the most pleasant weather. The wind was weak and contrary so that we made little headway.

The 23rd of August - With bright weather we had very high seas, which at times beat over the ship. We saw some sharks today.

The 24th of August - The sea was very calm, the weather was pleasant, and the wind weak. Therefore our journey went slowly. A ship loaded with ammunition, which separated from the fleet on the night of the nineteenth, was brought back to the fleet today by the frigate *Unicorn.* The ship's captain had planned to take it into an enemy American harbor. The captain and mate were immediately placed in arrest on a warship.

The 25th of August - The sea was exceptionally calm, but the water was very hot, as it has been for the last fourteen days. [The men] on our horse ship *Diana* caught a shark today. The jaws started low and went upward, and were so large that it could swallow a man.

The 26th of August - The water and the weather were stormy, and the wind contrary.

The 27th of August - As yesterday.

The 28th of August - The same.

<u>The 29th of August</u> - It was exceptionally warm weather with a contrary wind. Two ships, one of which was a warship, came from America and sailed through our fleet *en route* to Europe.

The 30th of August - The weather was beautiful and very hot, the wind rather favorable, but weak. A shark accompanied our ship for a time.

The 31st of August - As yesterday.

The 6th of September - Since the 31st [of August], nothing occurred. Due to our southerly course, it gets hotter each day. A two-masted ship from America sailed through our fleet. It was examined by the commodore and then continued on its way.

The 7th of September - The condition of the atmosphere changed. The weather was very sultry and close; the sea stormier than we had ever seen it before. Everything in the cabin began to be thrown about, if not made fast. At ten o'clock in the evening we had a severe thunderstorm, which lasted until one o'clock at night. This was the second one since 11 June.

The 8th of September - The wind was contrary, the weather pleasant and not too hot.

The 9th of September - As yesterday.

The 10th of September - Very hot weather during a wind calm.

Fire broke out on a transport ship loaded with Waldeckers. Because of the wind calm, boats from [other] ships could go to help, and in a few minutes, sixty boats were on hand, and with their help the fire was extinguished. It had started in a storeroom when a keg of rum caught fire, but fortunately was put out in time. At three o'clock this afternoon 1st Lieutenant Lange of the Wissenbach Regiment was buried at sea from the transport ship *Peternella.*

The 11th of September - We had good weather and favorable wind. While raising a sail, a rope broke so that one of our sailors, who was 76 years old and who from his youth had spent his entire life aboard ship, had the misfortune to fall into the ocean, and to drown before our eyes.

Today we saw a great many dolphins and flying fish. The dolphin is a very beautiful fish. In the water it takes on all colors, especially green, red, and yellow. He is the enemy of the flying fish. As soon as the dolphin gets near them, a great many of them spring out of the water, and return at another place, with the dolphin chasing them in the water. The dolphins weigh about ten pounds and much more. The flying fish, however, weigh about a quarter pound, or even less. They fly with their fins.

The 12th of September - We had quite favorable wind with very warm weather.

The wife of Grenadier [Friedrich] Ernst, of Captain Hessenmueller's Company, gave birth to a son. Whole schools of flying fish were seen today.

The 13th of September - The weather and wind were like yesterday. Wherever we looked, many large fish were to be seen, following the small flying fish.

The 14th of September - The child born day before yesterday was baptized. The non-commissioned officers spent this afternoon dancing and relaxing.

The 16th of September - The sea was very rough and a severe storm with strong wind sprang up about six o'clock. It lasted until two o'clock in the night. It was so dark it was impossible to see ten yards from the ship. We were in great danger throughout the night of one ship ramming another.

The 17th of September - This morning the fleet was

widely scattered. The warships had considerable trouble getting them all back together.

The 18th of September - With warm weather, we had a wind calm.

The 19th of September - We saw many birds, which were similar to woodcocks, in large swarms. We told ourselves that they meant America was near.

The 20th - The wind veered to our favor from the northeast.

The 21st - The wind was as yesterday and brought fall weather.

The 22nd - A south wind brought warm weather. This morning we saw about 1,000 birds swimming around on the ocean. In addition to many dolphins, we saw another type of fish which the English call bonitos. Our superintendent was able to catch two of them today, with a hook and line. One of eighteen pounds was enjoyed in our cabin this evening as a delicacy.

The 23rd of September - The wife of an artillery servant named Gerlach, gave birth to a son aboard our ship today, which was the second one [born during the voyage]. Toward evening, a flying fish which weighed about a quarter pound, fell on our ship. It appeared similar to a white fish. In flight his fore fins were spread.

The 24th of September - Again today, a child was baptized on board our ship. The weather was very hot.

The 25th of September - This morning was very stormy, and several ships lost the tops of masts.

The 26th of September - It was still stormy and rainy weather. This morning the ships were widely scattered, and we had to wait a long time before they were again assembled.

The 27th of September - During the past night we had a nearly full-blown storm. Everything in the ship flew about. Toward noon, two of our warships brought a ship to our fleet. We recognized it as a French ship by the white flag. After being closely examined by the commodore, it resumed its course to the east at evening. Again today, one of our sailors died. Scurvy is very prevalent among the sailors, and also among the soldiers.

The 28th of September - The weather was very hot. A third sailor died of scurvy this morning. One of our warships was missing since yesterday afternoon. At eleven o'clock tonight, the ship's captain came into the cabin and gave us the surprising news that enemy ships were nearby. By means of a cannon shot and the raising of some lanterns, the admiral or commodore gave a signal at the same time for all the ships to draw closer together. As the ship's captain had no cannon, he requested Lieutenant Colonel Koehler to load our regimental cannon which were then secured on our foredeck. This was done. As our artillerists were unfamiliar with this method of handling the guns, it required nearly a quarter hour to accomplish this. This made me feel that no favorable defense would be made if we had the misfortune to become separated from the fleet, and were attacked by a privateer. After the commodore examined the sloop [There appears to be a portion of the text missing as there has been no previous reference to a sloop.] it took a course to Europe.

The 29th of September - During the night, the third woman on our ship gave birth to a son. This noon an English merchant ship passed through our fleet, coming from Jamaica in the West Indies and bound for England.

The 30th - The warship missing since the 28th, the frigate *Unicorn*, rejoined this morning and brought a captured American privateer. The privateer, called *Wolf*, had ten cannons and sixteen swivels, and ninety men on board. It sailed from Boston on the 23rd of this month, and carried provisions for three months. Four of the captives came aboard our ship. They looked very shabby and had little baggage with them. I must note here, that neither this baggage nor any money was ever taken from anyone captured aboard a ship.

The 6th of October - Until now nothing has happened. Last night we passed many submerged rocks and therefore had to be careful not to run upon them. Again during the night, a sailor died. The scurvy among the men is so rampant, that few among them can perform their duty. It is no wonder this disease is raging among the soldiers, although proportionately it is not so prevalent as among the sailors. Since the first of this month we have had continuously favorable wind, but it is often very weak.

The 7th to the 9th of October - We tacked in the vicinity of Long Island on the American coast, but still could not see land. We received news from a warship that the 1st Division had landed. We could not have heard any better news, as we now believed we would soon join them, and get out of our present critical situation. Our discomfort aboard ship was made all the worse by the heat. The water had become so bad that when a keg was opened on deck it was necessary not to stand down wind so as not to be driven away by the stench. This evening, however, our joy about the anticipated landing was once again crushed. Instead of steering directly for Long Island, as noted by our charts, we suddenly changed our course from west to south.

The 10th of October - We continued our course toward the south, but continued to hope for the sight of land. Another grenadier, Wolff, of Captain Bode's Company, died today. The day was passed with rather depressed spirits, and nothing was heard but complaints and muttering, while each discussed the plans that had been made for landing. With some, it had gone so far that they even thought the commodore, by tacking about, was trying to play one, or more, of our ships into the enemy's hands.

The 15th of October - Tonight, two frigates joined our fleet, which, with their lanterns displayed, caused us much concern as we saw them while still at a distance. The appearance was taken as a sign that the often repeated plan was about to be carried out, as this could be nothing other than enemy ships. Everyone awaited an attack during the morning.

The 16th - At daybreak everyone saw the English flags flying on these ships. At nine o'clock, to our great joy, the commodore and several transport ships raised flags to indicate that land had been seen. Toward one o'clock in the afternoon, we saw some low hills to the north. It is doubtful that Columbus could have had greater joy upon catching his first glimpse of the New World, than we had. At once, everyone seemed to come alive. The sick allowed themselves to be brought on deck so as to be convinced of this discovery. Still, another sailor died.

The 17th of October - Because of a wind calm we did not sail very far today. We were so close to land, however, that we dropped anchor at evening.

The 18th of October - Due to the wide-spread scurvy among the sailors, we were only able to get underway this morning with the greatest effort. The land to the west, which we had lain near during the night, was the province of New Jersey, between the Delaware River and New York. After we finally, with great effort, got the ship underway, with the help of the soldiers, we steered to the north toward Long Island. Due to contrary wind we were unable to enter New York Harbor, however, and to our gret disgust found it necessary to put out the anchor at twelve o'clock, near Sandy Hook. Sandy Hook is a small, uninhabited sand island, on which a lighthouse stands, used as a reference for ships sailing to New York. A river divides it from the province of New Jersey.

The 19th of October - We weighed anchor at six o'clock this morning, and entered the channel between Long Island and Staten Island. It leads to New York. We saw a Hessian camp on Staten Island. On both islands, pleasant estates were to be seen. We dropped anchor toward seven o'clock, in the dark of night, in the North River, near New York. As the wind was not the best for entering [the harbor] today, most of the fleet remained lying at Sandy Hook, which is thirty miles from New York.

The 20th of October - Everyone gathered happily on the deck today, but instead of a beautiful city, we saw nothing but the ruins of beautiful houses. We lay at the west end of the city, where the rebels themselves had laid 300 houses in ashes after the city fell into our hands. At noon today the rest of our fleet joined us with the incoming tide. Despite our long journey, we had to consider ourselves lucky that we had not had a prolonged storm, and the entire fleet of 63 ships arrived here without a single loss. In this harbor we encountered more than 400 large, and numerous small, ships. New York is a large city, which is said to have had more than 5,000 houses before the fire. Some of the streets are straight, others are built in an irregular manner. It is well-situated for trade. Merchant ships can pull up to the wharves and unload their cargo with ease. It is an island, called York Island, and on the south end thereof, the North and East Rivers come together. On the point of the waterfront lies Fort George. The rebels had thrown up trenches and redoubts everywhere, of which they made no use, however, because our army made the descent on the rear of this island. The city makes an appearance of monotony and drabness, because most of the inhabitants had fled from fright, and in whole streets the houses stood empty, and have since been turned into barracks. New York had eighteen churches and meeting houses, the most splendid being St. Paul's Church and George's Chapel. Two of the eighteen were consumed in the fire. There was also a beautiful college, which at the present time has been converted to a hospital for the army. There is a royal dockyard here, but no new ships can be built, and only old ones are repaired. The region outside New York is quite pleasant. Two grenadiers died today.

The 21st - We still lay at anchor.

The 22nd - Finally, today the deeply wished for moment arrived, we left our residence of 142 days, in which we had put up with so much fear, distress, and many sad hours. We were loaded onto a sloop, and for a time everyone seemed melancholy, as if mutually recalling all the dangers from which we had been released. We sailed in the East River between Long and York Islands until we came to a whirlpool, where there were large rocks. The passage between these rocks is very narrow, and dangerous. It is called Hellgate. Here many old remnants of wrecked ships are to be seen. The channel is so narrow that objects can be thrown to land on either side of the ship. However, with favorable wind transport ships and frigates can sail through with ease. The master of our sloop told us that when our troops landed here, a boat with British grenadiers and artillery had gone under.

Note - Sir James Wallace, in the year 1778, sailed through Hellgate with the warship *Experiment*. 50 guns.

We traveled about fourteen English miles today and during the evening lay at anchor. This would not have been necessary if we had not found it necessary to stop on land twice because the master of our schooner did not know [the area].

The 23rd of October - We weighed anchor this morning at daybreak, and were landed on solid ground at New Rochelle at ten o'clock. General [William] Howe was in camp about three miles from here. Here we met the other troops from the 2nd Division, which had come from Europe with us. They had come in flatboats and landed before we did. We had to leave our baggage behind on the ships and were permitted to take nothing with us but our tents. After all the troops had landed, four two-horse wagons were delivered for transporting the tents. (Nothing more could possibly be loaded thereon.) We began our march to New Rochelle (actually in the direction of the church.) After marching several miles we had to pass in review before Lieutenant General [Leopold Philipp] von Heister. Although we only marched three English miles, many troops dropped out from fatigue. Near the church at New Rochelle we entered camp in the army line. This place is a French colony settled here with permission of the English. The whole colony is divided into farms, which are scattered about. It belongs to the province of New York. The Jaeger Company which landed with us today, had an engagement with the rebels already this evening, and Lieutenant [Karl] Rau was severely wounded in the leg. Most of the surrounding region has been laid waste by the rebels.

The 24th - We remained in camp.

The 25th - We received orders at daybreak to break camp and be prepared to march. The whole army marched away from us, and toward noon the 2nd Division, commanded by Lieutenant General von Knyphausen reentered our former camp. To deceive the enemy, the tents were set up in two lines so that our front was as long as it was yesterday. Due to a sharp cannonade near the army, which was to our right, we had to fall out this evening, but nothing more occurred.

The 26th - We remained in the previous location and received provisions for the second time. Each man received daily one pound of zwieback or wheat flour, one pound of beef or three-fourths of a pound of salt pork, one and one-third gill of rum equal to one and on-third small tankards or one-twelfth of a Maas. Two and one-half pence sterling were withheld from our pay for these items.

The 27th - We had a day of rest. The region seems rather fertile. Raising livestock is presently, despite many having already been taken away, in good condition. The inhabitants, of whom few are encountered in their homes, all seem to have lived in an ideal condition. The houses are beautiful and well-built, but not in the manner of our farmhouses. All the vacated houses had fine furnishings, which were ruined, and from which it can be seen that the residents had better tastes than the German farmers. The produce in this area is wheat, oats, Indian or Welsh corn, potatoes, flax, and buckwheat. There is also some rye, but in small amounts. There are pumpkins by the acre. The usual European garden vegetables have already been harvested, but traces of them are still found to show that such has been grown here. There is fruit of all sorts, except plums, in large amounts here, and especially a lot of peach trees. There are various types of trees, such as nuts, deciduous, cedar, acacia, tulip trees, beech, white beech, elder, willow, and a great many others, which I do not know, also chestnut. There are many chestnuts found here, from which we gather the ripe fruit in camp in the morning. Many of the flowers and bushes are completely unknown to us. The inhabitants' knowledge of botany is very limited and frequently they can not tell us the names of common trees. Only occasionally birch and linden are found here and there, of which the linden is similar in appearance of the trunk and leaves, but has a black mulberry. Wild cherry trees, the fruit of which grows like a grape and is black and as large as a pea, abound. The wood is supposedly very good for finishing by cabinet makers, and is especially good for use by gun makers.

The 28th - The corps commanded by Lieutenant General von Knyphausen, consisting of the Koehler Grenadier Battalion, and the Wutgenau, Stein, Wissenbach, Huyn, and Buenau Regiments, and the Waldeck Regiment marched from New Rochelle to Mile Square. The march was about six English miles. The road was bad and stony. The houses which we passed were all empty and in disrepair. We were to the rear of General Howe's army.

The 29th - A day of rest at Mile Square. This is a hilly region and it was necessary to set up camp on several hills.

The 30th - At nine o'clock yesterday evening, 1st Lieutenant von Romrodt, of the Wutgenau Regiment, was ordered on a command with 300 men of that regiment. They marched out of camp at midnight. About three o'clock in the morning, the entire corps, commanded by Lieutenant General von Knyphausen moved out, and an hour after daybreak arrived at a height on the east side of Kingsbridge. *En route* many burnt-out huts were seen, which had been built in the form of barracks. On the previously mentioned height, 1st Lieutenant von Romrodt and his command had occupied a fort which the enemy had vacated tonight. It was rather large, at least 900 to 1,000 men would be needed to defend it. The enemy had left cannons and ammunition behind. The fort had other additional small redoubts which we marched past on the right and left this morning. Fort Independence covers the entire region, and is especially laid out to cover the crossing from Kingsbridge on the land side to this side. A creek runs through the hills and cliffs about three-quarters of a mile from here, which joins the North or Hudson River and the East River. Both rivers and this creek create an island, called York Island, on which New York City lies. A small wooden bridge, called Kingsbridge, connects the mainland and this island, and gives the region its name;. The enemy is now engaged in tearing down this bridge to hinder our crossing to York Island. They are also taking the magazines from both sides of the bridge to their camp at Fort Washington. This fort lies about two and one-half miles in a direct line from us to the highest point, one could say cliff, on York Island. The area surrounding is covered with thick woods, marshes, and stony cliffs. Nature has provided far more defense than the art of fortification. The enemy say it is unconquerable, but it appears as if our present position is for the purpose of capturing the fort, so it remains to be seen how long this saying is true.

The 31st - We remained in camp on the height of Fort Independence. The Kingsbridge destroyed by the rebels, was repaired during the night, and Captain Neumann, of our battalion, crossed the Harlem Creek over the Kingsbridge this morning with 100 men and drove the enemy outposts back to the woods near Fort Washington. He then established himself securely on a height on the other side of the bridge.

The command which crossed the Harlem Creek today, sent some of their lightly wounded back.

The 1st of November - We remained in camp. Our provisions had to be brought from New Rochelle.

The 2nd of November - This morning our battalion marched over Kingsbridge and entered camp on a height. Fort Washington now lies a bit more than a mile from us.

The 3rd of November - The Koehler Grenadier Battalion outposts were engaged throughout the day with enemy patrols and suffered three men wounded.

The 4th of November - Three more men of the Koehler Grenadier Battalion were wounded at the outposts. Today the entire battalion moved into a woods, on the right, lying before the camp, which the enemy had previously occupied, but then found it necessary to leave in order to draw nearer to the abatis at Fort Washington. The tents for our battalion were left standing. The Wutgenau and Stein Regiments crossed Kingsbridge today, also. When the Stein Regiment was about to make camp on a level area in front of our camp, the enemy began to bombard it with a heavy fire from Fort Washington. This made it necessary for the regiment to withdraw from the designated place and to move behind a height occupied by the Wutgenau Regiment.

The 5th of November - Today the Wissenbach Regiment occupied the camp of the Koehler Grenadier Battalion. At eight o'clock in the evening, the Koehler Grenadier Battalion was relieved by a mixed command of all regiments, and entered camp on the right wing of the Wutgenau and Stein Regiments. Today several men were again severely wounded.

The 6th of November - We remained in place. The outposts were continually engaged.

The 16th of November - From the sixth until today, nothing more occurred, except that daily we suffered killed and wounded at the outposts. The entire army commanded by General Howe came from White Plains and entered camp the other side of Kingsbridge, on the height behind Fort Independence. A battery with heavy cannons was established on the height, opposite Fort Washington. Early this morning, at daybreak, a detachment of jaegers under the command of Captain [Friedrich Heinrich] Lorey, and the following regiments: Koehler Grenadier Battalion, Wutgenau, Lossberg, Knyphausen, Rall, Huyn, Buenau, and under the command of Lieutenant General von Knyphausen, marched into the woods which lay to the right of our camp and on the North River. The Stein Regiment occupied a redoubt to the left on a plain. The nine regiments, battalions, and corps listed above formed for the mass attack at the edge of these woods, at about seven o'clock. The many and strong abatis and swamps made it necessary for them to remain in place until about ten o'clock, before they could clear space enough to get through. At ten o'clock the main attack began against a stony cliff covered with trees, which they had to occupy before they could go against the fort. By eleven o'clock they were masters of this cliff, where nature had formed a defensive point, or more nearly, a breastwork, between the cliff and Fort Washington. This had been occupied by the rebels with cannons, without revetments. This breastwork was quickly overrun, but not without great loss on our side, especially by the Wutgenau Regiment, because the greatest part of the left flank of this corps was outflanked by cannons on the cliff, firing grapeshot. [Not known as such at that time.] As soon as this point, called the Stone Redoubt, was in our hands, we halted. In addition to the corps commanded by Lieutenant General von Knyphausen, the fort was fired upon by several frigates lying in the North River, and attacked from the side toward New York by a division of Englanders brought over the Harlem Creek in flatboats, and who made a descent below Laurel Hill. The fire from all sides was very heavy until the Stone Redoubt was taken, and then suddenly ceased. The [rebel] troops halted here and began to surrender. During the afternoon the fort capitulated and the occupants were made prisoners of war. The number of those captured amounted to more than 3,000, and the loss on our side, from the time of crossing over Kingsbridge to the surrender of the fort, in dead and wounded, amounted to nearly 400 men. The Koehler Grenadier Battalion had 38 men dead and wounded, of that number.

The 17th - The prisoners were sent to Harlem, where a Hessian hospital was established.

The 18th - The Koehler Grenadier Battalion and the Stein and Wissenbach Regiments moved into camp at Fort Washington. Several English regiments and the Wutgenau, Ditfurth, Leib, Prince Charles, Huyn, and Buenau Regiments marched to New York and set up camp near the city. They also received orders to submit embarkation lists.

The 19th of November - Lord [Charles] Cornwallis crossed the North River with a corps. The other three grenadier battalions, Linsing, Block, and Minnigerode, and two jaeger companies constituted the Hessian units that crossed over.

The 21st - According to general orders disseminated today, Fort Washington will be called Fort Knyphausen in the future.

The 19th of December - Since the last date, the Stein and Wissenbach Regiments and the Koehler Grenadier Battalion have remained in camp at Fort Knyphausen. In the meantime work on barracks has been constantly performed for the units assigned there. However, the grenadier battalion received orders today to march to New York tomorrow. All the other regiments, battalions, and corps have, in part, entered winter quarters, in part, cantonment quarters.

The 20th of December - The Koehler Grenadier Battalion was relieved by the Truembach Regiment, which came from New York. The first entered the quarters in New York vacated by the mentioned regiment. This evening we received orders to be prepared to embark tomorrow.

The 21st of December - The previously mentioned grenadier battalion embarked, the staff on the transport ship *Acolus*, Captain Bode's and Captain Hessenmueller's Companies on the ship *Symetry*, and Captain Neumann's and Captain Hohenstein's Companies on the ship *Royal Exchange.*

The 22nd of December - At eight o'clock this morning our ships departed and we set a course for Perth Amboy, but anchored at Prince's Bay on Staten Island.

The 27th of December - We remained lying at anchor at Prince's Bay until today. We have had to put up with a great deal these days. The weather was very cold and continuously stormy so that it was necessary to put out three anchors to prevent the ship from breaking loose. The Second Christmas Day was the worst for us as we expected the storm to tear us loose at any moment. Our sorrow was made all the worse because we had no food with us. We had been told at New York that we would debark on the 23rd or 24th, and it was not necessary to take provisions with us, as these would be left behind when we landed. Relying on this, we had taken nothing more with us than was necessary for the ships' needs until the 23rd. Unfortunately, they had taken no provisions, either, and we had to tolerate these miserable conditions until today, when the wind eased and we received fresh provisions from Perth Amboy. Here in Amboy we received the news that Colonel Rall's Brigade had been captured on the 26th of this month at Trenton. We asked here in Amboy about our horses, which were being brought in a separate sloop from New York by four servants. However, no one could provide any information.

The 28th of December - The battalion was landed today at South Amboy in Jersey. No troops had been in this region. We marched almost all day in heavy woods. The region was lightly developed, and here and there, with the exception of a few houses, some wretched huts were to be found which had been placed on new farms. During the evening we entered the small village called Spotswood, where we were quartered. There was an excellent forge here.

The 29th - We marched in as pitiful a region as yesterday, from Spotswood to New Brunswick on the Raritan River. Despite our belief that we had orders to be quartered here, we learned that we had to march ten English miles farther to Hillsborough. We joined three English regiments there, which were part of Colonel

[Charles] Mawhood‘s Brigade As these already occupied all the houses of the village, the battalion had to settle for barns.

The 30th - A day of rest at Hillsborough.

The 31st - We made cantonment quarters in the houses on the east side of the Mill’s River.

1777

The 1st of January - Instead of entering the new cantonment quarters as expected, we received orders tonight to move out at once. At two o'clock at night, the three English regiments and our grenadier battalion marched to Princeton. The baggage remained in Hillsborough. The three English regiments remained under the command of Colonel Mawhood in Princeton. The Koehler Grenadier Battalion joined Colonel [Carl Emil Ulrich von] Donop's Brigade in Trenton.

The 3rd - General [George] Washington marched to Princeton and attacked Colonel Mawhood, who lost many men from the three regiments which he had with him. Today a grenadier of the Koehler Grenadier Battalion was shot dead and another man wounded.

The 4th - The corps commanded by Lord Cornwallis marched back from Trenton today to New Brunswick on the Raritan. The corps consisted of sixteen battalions and regiments, and two companies of jaegers. All these troops entered winter quarters in a line about four miles long on both sides of the Raritan, which, taking the many troops into consideration, must be terrible. All the officers of the Koehler Grenadier Battalion were in two rooms. Small redoubts were constructed in the Brunswick area.

The 4th of January [sic] - Brunswick is an open place, built in a rectangle and pleasantly situated with many fine houses. The number of houses amounts to about 150. Single and two-masted ships can approach the wharf here. When it is flood tide, a sloop with 20 cannons can go close to the city. About an English mile up the Raritan River lies Raritan Landing, where a wooden bridge spans the river. The tide enters that far.

Copper mines are located near Brunswick, but at the present time these are not being worked. They belong to a local family, named French.

The rebel army had drawn in around us, and taken cantonment quarters which could constantly harass our outposts from all sides, and often did so. General Washington had his headquarters at Morristown. They were in the hills and were covered by strong defenses on all sides. We had no other posts in Jersey, except Perth Amboy, which lies at the point where the Raritan River exits. It is about sixteen or eighteen miles from Brunswick. However, we had no communications with the corps there, except that provided by strong detachments which had to be taken from troops outside our area, when the opportunity arose. The only communications between New York and Amboy are carried on by water, but even this is uncertain because the enemy patrols on land often attack the ships.

If I exclude two unprofitable excursions, or more accurately, sallies, to Bound Brook, the entire winter was spent on the defensive, except to acquire forage. For our purpose it was often necessary to send out five or six regiments in order to dislodge the enemy. Duty for the troops was extremely difficult and very hard. Everyone who went on duty had to sleep under the open sky. Snow fell often, and it was deep, and it seemed colder to us here than in Europe. Except for the delivered provisions, there was nothing for the troops to buy. When the miserable and wretched quarters are considered with this, it is easy to understand why sickness could not be kept down. These evils hit the Koehler Grenadier Battalion especially hard. This unit consisted of young people only, who still suffered from scurvy from the ship. Because of the cold, the scurvy returned and became an illness. Because the number of sick increased everyday, and because of the circumstances, that those convalescing in the hospital in New York, often had to remain there for a month, before they had an opportunity to return to the battalion, the duty for those still healthy, became even more frequent. This caused them to become sick, until finally it reached a point where the battalion was no longer able to perform duty like the other grenadier battalions.

The 10th of May - To the present nothing has changed, except that nearly everyday we were alarmed and disturbed, especially the Hessian jaeger companyies, which had the outposts toward Bound Brook, and Quibbletown. At about five o'clock today a heavy cannon and small arms fire was heard toward Piscataway, on the road to Perth Amboy. Not only was it very heavy, but it continued for a long time. The 42nd Regiment (Scots) had planned to attack the enemy in his quarters, but was beaten back with a loss of 50 men, killed and wounded. This regiment had previously lost 36 men dead, wounded, and captured, including the major, who was wounded.

The 11th of May - The garrison from Bound Brook and surrounding places made an attack on the Jaeger Company and the English Guards, but also found it necessary to fall back with losses. We now hear from the prisoners and deserters that during yesterday's attack, a misunderstanding arose. According to one account, the enemy had decided to make a general attack on Bound Brook this morning at four o'clock, because the side toward Princeton was most strongly occupied by us. A false attack was to be made there, and to accomplish the main object, they meant to send their main force against Perth Amboy, on the other side, where we were weaker. They hoped to defeat our troops completely, or at least to force our side to retreat, which would naturally cause us considerable loss, and drive us into a corner.

The 16th of May - The forces in occupation in and around Brunswick, on both sides of the Raritan, pulled into camp on the heights. There is almost never a day when our outposts are not attacked by the enemy. We were now more clearly drawn together than during the winter, and the woods and fields, which have turned green, contribute to this impression.

The 5th of June - We received orders to hold ourselves ready for a planned embarkation. The spot where this is to take place has not yet been determined. Each battalion is to take no more than seven riding horses, and four wagons without horses.

The 6th of June - We were given the names of the transport ships which each battalion was assigned. The Koehler Grenadier Battalion received one called *Bird,* of 227 tons, and the *Twiet*, of 162 tons. Today a rebel captain, who had lived in Brunswick for some time as a spy, and during that time passed himself off as a merchant, was hanged on a tree close to our camp.

A letter, which he wrote to General Washington, and in which he promised to set fire to all the magazines in Brunswick on the King's birthday, the 4th of June, had been given for delivery to an English grenadier, who had promised to desert for a given amount of guineas. The grenadier, however, delivered it to Lord Cornwallis. The plan was exposed, that General Washington was ready the same day, as soon as the fires were set, to attack us. The enthusiasm of this spy was so great, that as he came to the ladder and was about to climb it, he pulled the white hood over his eyes, and said to the bystanders, "I die for liberty."

The 9th of June - The first recruits of Lieutenant [Friedrich A.J.] von Wangenheim's transport joined us in Brunswick.

The 12th of June - The commanding general-in-chief, Sir William Howe, and Lieutenant General von Heister, with many English regiments, and Major General [Johann Daniel] von Stein's Brigade, consisting of the Leib Regiment, the Donop and Mirbach Regiments, and the Combined Battalion [remnants of Rall, Knyphausen, and Lossberg Regiments, after the Battle of Trenton] arrived in Brunswick. As soon as the regiments entered camp, many defensive positions were thrown up on both sides of the Raritan River.

The 13th of June - Many flatboats came up the Raritan River from New York. In each flatboat was a wagon which could be put in the water easily, and the boat was then loaded on it. In a short time, the boats which arrived on the water were seen moving on the land. At nightfall, the army began the march to Princeton, but then halted at the Mills River in the region of Hillsborough. The rebels had entered the hills on the other side of the Mills River, and fortified the area. Several English regiments, the Koehler Grenadier Battalion, and the Combined Battalion remained in Brunswick, under the command of General [Edward] Mathew.

The 19th of June - The army returned here without having undertaken anything against the enemy.

The 20th - According to orders received yesterday, this morning our battalion moved out with Major General [John] Vaughan, and escorted the flatboats on wagons to Perth Amboy. We met two jaeger companies, newly arrived from Hesse, and two Ansbach-Bayreuth regiments, and the Waldeck Regiment.

The 22nd - The entire army arrived from New Brunswick, and entered camp on the height near us. The English Light Infantry suffered forty dead and wounded today, in the rear guard. The region between Brunswick and Amboy is a solid woods, and ideal for the rebel method of fighting. Between the two places lies the small, pleasant village of Bonhamtown. Six English regiments and Major General Stein's Brigade embarked today, and went to Staten Island, where they will board transport ships. At Amboy today, Lieutenant General von Heister received orders recalling him to Hesse. He also transferred to Staten Island in order to go to New York.

The 25th of June - The six embarked English regiments and Stirn's Brigade came to Amboy on their transport ships, and were landed this evening.

The 26th - The army moved out again and marched in several columns to Brunswick, to attack the rebels who had moved out of their defensive camp. After the loss of sixty prisoners, many dead, and the loss of three metal cannons, they pulled back into the hills. Many of us died from the heat. When the advantage of this last expedition is considered, being able to cross the North River, the loss on both sides seems to balance. Several of the regiments which returned from the expedition were embarked yet today. The Minnigerode Grenadier Battalion captured two of the three metal cannons mentioned. Today a large part of the army's baggage was transferred to Staten Island.

The 28th - General Howe returned from the expedition with the army. Several English regiments and the Leib and Mirbach Regiments were immediately embarked on the transport ships that were present. Some English regiments and the Linsing, Lengercke, and Minnigerode Grenadier Battalions were transferred to Staten Island today.

The 30th of June - At three o'clock this afternoon, the Light Infantry and the Hessian Jaegers, which constituted the rear guard, also came here, across the North River. With this, we completely evacuated the Province of New Jersey, which was of little use to us, and had cost many lives. Perhaps it would have been better, if we had not gone there, or if we had stayed. The enemy's light cavalry was already in Perth Amboy before the last boat left. Unquestionably, New Jersey is one of the most fruitful and splendid provinces in North America. There are many fertile and splendid farms there, and everything necessary to nourish people is produced in an over-abundance. However, it is far short of the necessary people to develop the province. It could easily support four times as many people as it has. There are still large and under-developed regions where there is nothing but forests, and no trace of improvement is to be found, except that provided by nature. Perth Amboy had several beautiful houses. The city's situation is exceptionally pleasant, because it is built on a gradually sloping hill, and the view from every part of the city is wonderful. It lies on a peninsula made by an arm of the North River, the Kills, and the Raritan River. Looking to the south, across a great bay, Sandy Hook can be seen in the open sea. Amboy still does not have many houses, but the streets are all laid out in a uniform manner. It is well-situated for trade, as merchant and transport ships can come up to the wharf.

The 2nd and 3rd of July - The army on Staten Island began a march. This proceeded very slowly as there is only one road on Staten Island which runs from the southwest to the northeast, along which we had to march. This road is seventeen miles long, which is the length of Staten Island. Near Cole's Ferry, opposite New York, we entered camp. This place is also called the Watering Place because the ships take on water here.

The 6th of July - Lieutenant General [Henry] Clinton arrived from England in a frigate which escorted eight transport ships.

The 7th, 8th, and 9th - The designated troops for the expedition were embarked on the fleet lying here. The fleet, counting the warships and all the other ships, contained 300 to 400 ships. It is the largest fleet the inhabitants of this region have ever seen. Staten Island is rather well-developed and has many hills and fresh water springs.

The 14th of July - The Koehler Grenadier Battalion and two English regiments broke camp at Cole's Ferry, and were transferred to New York. From Cole's Ferry to New York is ten miles. Two miles beyond New York, we entered camp on Greenwich Road..

The 15th of July - The general order was given that everyone going with the fleet on the sixteenth should go aboard. Lieutenant General von Heister went on board in order to return to Europe.

The 16th - We moved out from Greenwich, passed Fort Knyphausen about noon, crossed Kingsbridge, and arrived at the height where Fort Independence lies on the road to Marosing. We noted many newly-built redoubts on these heights. General [Martin] Schmidt commanded the Hessian regiments here, namely, the Truembach, Prince Charles, Stein, and Wissenbach Regiments, and the Koehler Grenadier Battalion. All the troops in this region and on Long and Staten Islands are commanded by General Clinton. Previously, Lieutenant General von Knyphausen commanded these posts. Later, however, he sailed with the embarked corps. York Island, which is almost one cliff after the other, had been greatly rebuilt since last fall, when it was totally in ruins. From New York to Kingsbridge is a distance of fourteen English miles, which is also the length of the island. However, at its widest point, it is only three miles across.

The 19th of July - The Koehler Grenadier Battalion marched over Kingsbridge, which it had to repair at the same time, and entered camp on the hill at Spitting Devil, on the North River, near the Truembach Regiment.

The 20th - We heard that the fleet had departed from Staten Island.

The 11th of September - Until today we have remained in this region, completely undisturbed. However, there has been constant activity erecting redoubts on the surrounding heights of the region, and repairing the existing ones. Today General Clinton took most of the troops camped on this island, and crossed the North River, at three different places, into Jersey. Of the Hessians, only the Prince Charles Regiment went with him.

The 13th and 14th of September - The troops which had gone into Jersey, returned, having accomplished nothing, but they brought some livestock back. Supposedly it was a diversion to give General [John] Burgoyne relief so that he can push on to Albany.

The 4th of October - Since the fourteenth of the previous month, we have remained undisturbed. At the start of this month a fleet arrived from Europe. In addition to the recruit transports, two Hessian jaeger companies, uniforms, and other campaign necessities arrived. Colonel [Wolfgang Friedrich] von Woellwarth commanded the transport. General Clinton went up the North River with a corps, on transport ships. Major General Schmidt marched at daybreak today to Mile Square with the following corps: Emmerich Chasseurs, the Stewart Grenadier Battalion, the Koehler Grenadier Battalion, the 35th Regiment, the Truembach Regiment, the York Volunteers, and the newly-arrived Hessian Jaegers.

The 5th of October - The above corps, minus the Hessian Jaegers, the Emmerich Chasseurs, and the Truembach Regiment, returned and entered the camp which had been left standing. Those units which did not return, were embarked on the North River, and sailed up to Fort Montgomery, where they joined General Clinton's corps.

The 12th of October - The Koehler Grenadier Battalion embarked below Spitting Devil on the transport ship *Union*, and followed the corps of Lieutenant General Clinton. The baggage was left behind, as were the tents. At Verplanck's Point, or King's Ferry, the transport ship *Union*, which had been joined by several others with the two regiments from Ansbach and the Waldeck Regiment, joined the fleet under the command of Commodore [William] Hotham, who was on board the *Preston*, 50 cannons. Fort Montgomery and several others, whose defense against capture or conquest depended upon the first, were already in our hands, having been taken by storm. About 300 men, including 23 officers, had been made prisoners by us during the capture of this fort. Also, the enemy had set fire to all of their armed ships, which had been lying in the North River, including several small frigates and row galleys, to prevent them from falling into our hands.

Because the North River gets narrower here, and has very high, steep banks, it is the key to the region farther up the Hudson River. For this reason, the enemy had strongly fortified it on both sides. A very strong iron chain had been stretched across the river. This fell into our hands and was taken to New York.

<u>The 14th of October</u> - The troops still aboard ship landed on the east side of the North River, and entered the camp from which the troops under the command of General Clinton had marched out. However, they only bivouacked because the baggage was not brought from the ship. We assumed we would proceed toward Albany, either to join General Burgoyne coming from Canada, or at least to give him some relief, because the corps under his command was

in difficulty, and had been surrounded by General [Horatio] Gates. It seemed our forward movement depended on reports from General Vaughan, who has gone farther up the North River with four English regiments. General [William] Tryon has already burned down all the enemy magazines, houses, armories, and barracks at Peekskill.

The 20th of October - A sloop-of-war came from Philadelphia with dispatches from General William Howe for Sir Henry Clinton. Immediately after the sloop arrived, orders were received for everyone to prepare to embark again. The start was made today.

The 22nd of October - After everyone was on board again, except for the corps under General Vaughan, and some who were on the west bank in New Jersey near Fort Montgomery, and busy demolishing it, part of the fleet again got under sail and returned to New York and Staten Island, including the Koehler Grenadier Battalion. Each regiment entered its former camp. The sudden change was necessitated by a relief force which General Howe had requested for Philadelphia.

The 27th - The corps, which had remained behind at Fort Montgomery, arrived at Kingsbridge on the North River. Of General Vaughan we have had no further news as to where he might be with the four English regiments.

The 10th to the 12th of December - All the regiments and corps, except the Koehler Grenadier Battalion, left camp and entered their designated winter quarters.

The 30th of December - The Koehler Grenadier Battalion moved out of camp at Kingsbridge and entered winter quarters in the barracks at Fort Knyphausen. The 45th Regiment and Bayard's Corps were already there. The commander was Major General Tryon.

The 31st of December - The Hereditary Prince Regiment, Prince Charles, Truembach, and Stein Regiments entered winter quarters in New York, the Wissenbach Regiment on the East River, and the recently arrived Mirbach Regiment, which suffered severely at Red Bank on 22 October, on the North River and at Greenwich. These were all the Hessian troops in the region. The Koehler Grenadier Battalion at that time had the misfortune to receive wretched winter quarters because the barracks were wretched. The battalion had to send a detachment of 100 men to Kingsbridge, where it was relieved every eight days, but had no other duty. The Wissenbach Regiment provided a detachment of 100 men at Fort Independence, which were also relieved every eight days. The four Hessian regiments in New York sent 400 men to McGowan's Pass, and they are relieved every four weeks.

Another year's campaigning is finished, and all that we have accomplished, with the loss of a great many men, is the taking of Philadelphia, as according to all reports, we have taken nothing else. In balance, the conquest of this single city without considering the many people lost during this expedition, and with those lost at Saratoga, and made prisoners by the truce, makes the scale tip in favor of the enemy. Only future developments will determine whether Philadelphia is of any value to us. It is much to be wished, and it would have been better, to capture New Jersey. Everyone here attributes the capture of the Northern Army to General Howe. Some even go so far as to claim it was in direct contradiction to the Ministry's plans that General Howe went to Philadelphia by such a round-about route, as he received orders to do nothing which would interfere with his uniting with the Northern Army. If this were true, which is much to be doubted, he utterly disregarded the orders, and instead of going north, he went south, and to such a great distance that it may have been General Howe's intention to draw the enemy away from the main point, and into a side issue. This would not only give him an advantage, and facilitate General Burgoyne's march, but tire the enemy and lead to his destruction.

1778

The 2nd of June - We remained absolutely peaceful in winter quarters, as regards the enemy and other changes, and nothing new has excited us. According to today's orders, Lieutenant General Clinton has been named commander-in-chief of the army, and Sir William Howe is returning to Europe.

The 15th of June - The troops in the region of Kingsbridge entered camp. The Hessian troops here are in the brigade of Colonel [Carl Wilhelm] von Hachenberg, and consist of the Koehler Grenadier Battalion and the Truembach Regiment.

July - Early this month the army from Philadelphia arrived in this region, having come through lower Jersey. All the troops marched by land to Sandy Hook, then went aboard ship, and were brought over here. The heavy baggage arrived here by water. The enemy harassed our troops constantly. The arriving troops were landed on York, Staten, and Long Islands, and entered camps there. Most, however, came to York Island, including the entire Hessian corps. The troops had barely landed when [Charles Hector], Comte d'Estaing arrived at Sandy Hook with a French fleet of eleven ships-of-the-line, not counting frigates, and blockaded the harbor. Our local fleet, commanded by Admiral [Richard, Lord] Howe, was in a bad situation, very weak, and could not attack the French, but had to adopt a defensive position. We remained in this situation fourteen days and anticipated an attack at any moment. Meantime, all the old ships were repaired and, as much as possible, prepared for the defense. It is said, that Count d'Estaing departed for Rhode Island without undertaking the least thing.

August - We finally received reports that Count d'Estaing intended to attack Rhode Island, and actually had already entered the harbor. Part of the land forces on board [the French ships] had landed on that island, and joined a considerable number of rebels who had crossed from the mainland onto Rhode Island, and placed our forces under a full and very tight blockade. Admiral Howe strengthened his fleet with as many old ships as he could outfit, and which had any resemblance to warships. General Clinton embarked an English corps, consisting primarily of light infantry and grenadiers, in order to sail up the Long Island Sound to Rhode Island.

A fortunate maneuver allowed Admiral Howe to accomplish his task. Although he had no intention of engaging the French, which according to rumor his fleet was in no condition to do, his arrival, even at a distance, gave Admiral d'Estaing such a fright, that he left the harbor at Rhode Island. A short time later, he again entered the harbor, but did not stay long nor accomplish anything of consequence. Instead he departed for the second time, and sailed to Boston. The [American] army followed the admiral's example, and withdrew to the mainland. Our troops attacked his rear guard during this retreat, losing many people in so doing, without, it is said, doing the enemy any material harm. Meantime, we continued to occupy Rhode Island, although we had to burn the entire fleet of frigates and other ships there, to prevent them falling into enemy hands.

The 24th of September - Until today, the troops have remained quietly in their camps on York, Long, and Staten Islands. General Lord Cornwallis crossed the North River to New Jersey today with a strong corps. Lieutenant General von Knyphausen marched over Kingsbridge to the heights near Philipse's House with another strong corps. All the troops bivouacked.

The 11th and 12th of October - The troops marched back into their previous camps, without having been harassed by the enemy. As soon as the army returned, a strong corps of Englanders was embarked under the command of Major General [James] Grant in order to go to the West Indies. The Seitz Regiment is to embark for Halifax.

The 26th of October - According to orders received yesterday, the grenadier battalion marched from Kingsbridge to New York today.

The 27th - This morning schooners carried the battalion across to Staten Island.

The 28th of October - The Koehler Grenadier Battalion occupied the huts that the Waldeck Regiment vacated when it embarked with General Grant's fleet. [Although General Grant went to the West Indies, the Waldeckers were part of a force which went to Pensacola.]

November - The end of this month, the Truembach and Wissenbach Regiments, the 71st Regiment of Highlanders, a battalion of light infantry, and several provincial corps embarked, it is said, to undertake an expedition to the southern provinces. The end of this month, the English 26th Regiment arrived on Staten Island and occupied the huts vacated by the 7th Regiment, on the right wing. On the right wing, there are two battalions of provincials of General [Cortland] Skinner's Brigade, in huts, and the 37th Regiment is in huts at Richmond. These troops are the entire force on this island. Major General [Alexander] Leslie is in overall command.

<u>December</u> - We worked until the end of this year building new huts and making repairs. The rebels often came in small parties from Jersey, at night, and secretly plundered isolated houses, especially those on the sound on the west end of the island, which was not occupied by us.

1779

January - To this point, we had spent the winter in our huts, very lonely, but peacefully. The cold caused much suffering because our huts faced the northwest wind, which is the sharpest and coldest in North America, and which prevails during the winter.

The 27 - Today the Koehler Grenadier Battalion received orders promoting our commander, Lieutenant Colonel Koehler, to colonel and transferring him to the Truembach Regiment. Major [Wilhelm] Graf of the Seitz Regiment in Halifax was named commander of our grenadier battalion, and the name was changed to Graf.

The 15th of March - Colonel Koehler left the grenadier battalion and Captain Hessenmueller, as senior captain, was ordered by Lieutenant General von Knyphausen to take command for the present.

At the end of the month, Major Graf arrived at the battalion, from Halifax, and assumed command.

The 17th of September - We remained peacefully, throughout the entire summer, in our huts on Staten Island. Today we received orders to be prepared to embark with the other three Hessian grenadier battalions, and to submit the required lists. In addition to the four grenadier battalions, 200 Hessian jaegers, two battalions of English grenadiers, two battalions of light infantry, the 7th, 23rd, 33rd, 37th, and 54th and 57th Regiments, the Queen's Rangers, Fanning's Corps, and the Volunteers of Ireland were ordered to embark.

The 19th of September - The order of the previous date was changed, and the Hessian grenadiers and jaegers were not to embark.

The 21st of September - Six of the mentioned English Regiments and the Queen's Rangers embarked today, but remained lying off Staten Island. Lieutenant General Cornwallis had command of these units.

The 28th of September - Two companies of the 44th Regiment were landed on the island. This Regiment embarked fourteen days ago with the Old Lossberg and Kynphausen Regiments, and went to sea during the equinox (23 September), in order to go to Canada. A transport ship, on which were troops of this regiment, sank. The ship on which Colonel [Johann] von Loos sailed, returned to port without a mast. During this same time, the ship commanded by Captain [Ernst Eberhard von] Altenbochum was captured by a privateer, but retaken by the English warship *Solebay*, and has now returned. A transport commanded by Captain [Ludwig August] von Hanstein is still missing. Two transport ships with the Kynphausen Regiment were captured by the rebels, and one of those taken to Philadelphia, and the other to Little Egg Harbor, according to news brought to us by people from New Jersey. The third transport ship for the regiment is still missing at this time. It was the worst time of the year for this departure, as the inevitable storms always appear at this season.

The 30th of September - The corps commanded by Lieutenant General Lord Cornwallis landed, but was ordered to remain ready to embark again at any moment. The landing supposedly took place because Admiral Count d'Estaing arrived in the southern provinces with a French fleet and army, and made a descent upon Savannah, in Georgia. Savannah and the troops in that place are reported in great danger. General [Augustine] Prevost, who had advanced as far as Charleston, to which place the troops commanded by General Cornwallis had been ordered, and who had called upon that city to surrender, upon receipt of this news, pulled back to Savannah in the greatest haste. It is even reported that after capturing Savannah, the French plan to visit us here. With this in mind, the old ships here are being repaired so they can be sunk in The Narrows to prevent the French from entering, should that fleet come here.

The 10th of October - The corps commanded by Lieutenant General Cornwallis was embarked again.

The 12th of October - They were again debarked because news came from the south that Savannah had actually been put under siege.

The 24th of October - We received orders that the Graf Grenadier Battalion and the other three Hessian grenadier battalions were to enter winter quarters in New York. The Landgraf Regiment is to occupy the huts occupied by the Graf Grenadier Battalion up to this time.

The 3rd of November - Instead of the Landgraf Regiment, the Buenau Regiment arrived and entered the huts of the Graf Grenadier Battalion.

The 5th of November - The Graf Grenadier Battalion embarked at Cole's Ferry, and was shipped over to New York. We had spent a year on this island in complete peace and good health. Several English regiments, including among others, the 47th Regiment, had to be relieved because of the many sick men, which prevented them from performing duty. It was also noteworthy that the Graf Grenadier Battalion lived for almost a full year in the wretched huts, and had no illness, possibly because these huts had a continuous fresh sea breeze.

The 18th of November - We were informed, in orders, that not only had the French and rebels formally placed Savannah under siege, but had actually stormed the defenses and been beaten back with severe losses. Our joy was all the greater as everyone had already given that place up, the entire province, and all the troops assigned there.

The 19th of November - This evening the entire New York garrison moved out, formed a line on the North River, and fired a *feu de joie* because of the victory at Savannah.

December - At the beginning of this month the grenadier brigade received orders to be prepared to embark, and the following assignments were made:

Linsing [Battalion] on *Kingston* and *Polly* - Blue [Division] - to display one red ball on the fore [mast].

Vacant [Battalion] on *Royal Briton* and *Amity's Providence* - Blue [Division] - to display two red balls on the main [mast].

Lengercke [Battalion] on *Two Sisters* and *Munificence* - Blue [Division] - to display one red ball on the main [mast].

Graf [Battalion] on *Caldonia, Corsica,* and *Eliza* - Blue [Division] - to display two red balls on the fore [mast].

Generals [Henrich Julian] von Kospoth and [Johann Christoph] von Huyn on the *Andrew*.

Hospital [ship] *Sally* to display one yellow [ball] at the foretop masthead.

The 19th of December - After all baggage was loaded, the troops also went on board today. The Graf Grenadier Battalion embarked on the above designated ships in the following manner:

The staff, artillery, and part of Captain Hohenstein's Company on the *Caledonia*.

Captain Bode's Company and part of Captain Neumann's Company on *Eliza*.

Captain Hessenmueller's Company and the remainder of Captain Neumann's and Captain Hohenstein's Companies on *Corsica*.

The Grenadier Brigade was relieved at New York

by Landgraf, Donop, and Leib Regiments.

The 22nd of December - About ten o'clock this morning, the ships in the East River weighed anchor and set sail. Near Governor's Island, our ship *Caledonia* was in danger of being run down by another, but the care and ability of our ship's captain, to our great joy, minimized this. Our nemesis suffered the loss of a stern corner from his ship and considerable rigging. At two o'clock in the afternoon, we anchored near Sandy Hook, where a fleet of 108 ships lay.

The 23rd of December - Today a fleet of more than 100 ships sailed for Europe from Sandy Hook. The Hessian invalids, commanded by Captain [Philipp Ludwig] Reichel, were in this fleet. A number of ships assigned to our fleet came from New York today and joined with us.

The 26th of December - The entire fleet gathered here at Sandy Hook, numbering at least 105 ships, went under sail today. Admiral [Mariott] Arbuthnot, on the *Europa*, 64 guns, commanded the fleet. In addition to the *Europa*, the *Russel*, 74 guns; *Robust*, 74 guns; *Raisonable*, 64 guns; *Defiance*, 64 guns; *Renown*, 50 guns; *Romulus*, 44 guns; *Roebuck*, 44 guns; and *Perseus*, 20 guns, sailed with the fleet.

Generals accompanying the fleet were: Commander-in-Chief Sir Henry Clinton, Lieutenant General Lord Cornwallis, Major General [James] Paterson, Major General Kospoth, and Major General von Huyn.

The following troops were embarked: Two battalions of English light infantry, two battalions of English grenadiers, the 7th, 23rd, 33rd, 63rd, and 54th Regiments, Captain [Patrick] Ferguson's Corps, the New York Volunteers, a detachment of the 71st Regiment, a detachment of the 17th Light Dragoon Regiment, a corps of engineers, a detachment of 250 Hessian jaegers commanded by Major [Ludwig Johann Adolf] von Wurmb, Captain [George, Lord Coleraine] Hanger's Chasseur Corps, the four Hessian grenadier battalions, the Huyn Regiment, and Captain [Johann Adam] Bauer of the Angelelli Regiment with recruits for that regiment, and the Wissenbach Regiment.

We sailed out with a most favorable wind, and before evening, had lost sight of land.

The 27th of December - This was a pleasant spring day. According to our ship's captain, we had already reached the Delaware Capes today, but because we are so far out to sea, we could not see them. At nightfall a strong south-southeast wind arose, which developed into a full-blown storm by midnight.

The 28th of December - The storm continued and the night was sad for us. We began to receive the unpleasant effects of winter voyage.

The 29th - Toward noon the wind letup and the storm abated. The fleet, which was widely scattered, was brought together again by the warships. A warship had taken the transport *Anna*, on which were Captain Hanger's Chasseurs in tow, and brought it back. This transport ship had lost its middle mast in the storm. The storm had driven us back a great distance.

The 30th of December - At noon our ship's captain took a sighting. According to his reckoning, we were at 37°47' north latitude. It is obvious, however, that this observation is incorrect, considering that the last storm drove us backward.

The 31st of December - We had pleasant weather on a rather restless sea.

1780

The 1st of January - New Year's Day was a pleasant spring day. We sailed on a fairly smooth sea. According to the noon observation, we were at 34°06' north latitude.

The 2nd of January - Yesterday's calm weather changed into a strong storm tonight. The wind and waves raged continuously in the most frightful manner. The waves often went over our ship and we always expected one to swamp us. A large iron pot, a large case, and a large piece of iron torn loose by the storm, made the danger more eminent by rolling back and forth, as no one dared enter where these items were. One of our sailors, who was sick, lost his life when the loose case rolled over him. As our ship was not very big, we were affected even more by the violence of the storm. Our situation was made worse because neither we nor the ship's captain was able to cook, which made all of us really sick. Including the ship's captain, we had only sixteen sailors, of whom one had already died. We also had to worry that if the storm continued for a long time, and the ship withstood it, and if the sailors became sick, then the duties would not be carried out as necessary, and we would naturally be in grave danger, because no job in the world is more dangerous than that of a sailor in a storm. In this situation, the English sailor is better than all others. The difference on our ship was that we had all come here from Europe with only German and Dutch sailors. While the latter showed their faintheartedness at the least danger, the courage of the English seemed to increase as the danger increased. The fleet was so scattered today that only two or three ships could be seen at times. When the waves, high as mountains, crashed angrily over the ship, it seemed each time as if we were hurrying to our destruction.

The 3rd of January - It was like yesterday and the night before last. The water poured in through every opening on the ship, and everyone had to be alert that it did not go below in the ship, and what ran upon the deck, ran off on the other side. The entire deck was often covered with water, and we did not dare open the ventilation ports or entrances to the cabins for fear that the water would enter the ship.

The 4th of January - The storm abated somewhat, and for the first time we could cook, although the cook had to be securely tied with ropes.

The 5th of January - The storm was as strong as yesterday.

The 6th - We had weather like yesterday's. To our complete surprise, we had completely lost the fleet last night, and saw not a single ship today. Therefore, we did not even know what course to steer. We had not only to fight the storm, but had to expect at any moment to fall into the hands of a privateer, as our ship did not have a single cannon on board with which to defend ourselves. The ship's captain and his entire crew seemed more concerned about this last danger than we were.

The 7th of January - The storm continued. To our great joy today we discovered the fleet, or at least some ships, and a warship. According to the noon observation, we were at 30° north latitude, or already past Charleston. True, we were far out to sea, because the storm had made it necessary, due to a contrary northwest wind, to sail far out to sea.

The 8th of January - The weather was like yesterdays.

The 9th of January - The storm began to slacken. Today we were at 30°02' north latitude.

The 10th of January - With an east wind, the storm changed into the most pleasant summer day. The fleet now consisted of only 54 ships, which were again close to one another. Fifty-one ships were missing, having become separated from us during the storm.

The 11th of January - The weather began to grow stormy again, and the sea began to run high due to a strong northwest wind. A great many fish, in schools, swam past the ship, which means an [approaching] storm according to the sailors. At noon we again had a full storm. All the sails but one were taken in. With this single sail, we cruised with very warm, sultry weather.

The 12th of January - The storm continued with bright sunshine. After taking today's observation, our captain assured us that we were already 31 miles south of Savannah, Georgia, but far out in the sea, away from the land. Because of a contrary northwest wind, we could not sail toward land, but were driven even farther out to sea.

The 13th of January - The storm still continued. Because of the contrary wind, we could do nothing but tack. Today was very cool, and it snowed. We did not know how far out to sea we had been driven.

The 14th - The storm abated, and the sea was rather calm. According to the noon observation, we were at 31°45' north latitude. The weather was still cold, but more bearable than yesterday. The continued northwest wind made it necessary for us to tack. We were again at the latitude of the South Carolina coast.

The 15th of January - It was a really pleasant day, with bright weather. Meantime, the contrary wind of yesterday continued, and we could do nothing but tack. Toward noon it became overcast, which prevented us from taking a noon observation of the height of the sun. A black land bird, the size of a turtle dove, with long black legs and a long black beak, flew to our ship. Thus, we knew we were near land, supposedly we are near Bermuda.

The 16th of January - We had yesterday's sailing, wind, and weather. During the afternoon, a ship loaded with supplies raised an emergency flag. Immediately, all the boats, on a signal from the admiral, gathered around the vessel in distress. The people and part of the stores were removed to the frigate *Perseus*. The ship was leaking, and at evening, was given over to the wind and waves. It was the *Swan*. At noon today, we were at 29°14' north latitude. At nightfall the weather turned stormy.

The 17th of January - We continued to tack in bright, but stormy weather. According to today's observation, we sailed at 30°03' north latitude. Four robin red breasts [sic](a bird like a German wine thrush) flew around the ship. From this, we can be sure we are near land, supposedly the islands of Bermuda.

The 18th of January - Due to the continued contrary wind, we still had to tack. By today's observation, we were at 30°11', or in the same region as yesterday.

The 19th of January - This morning the admiral and Agent Tomkins made the signal for all transport ship captains to transfer the troops from one transport ship to others, immediately. The ship was also called the *Swan*, and had light infantry on board; most of whom were placed on board the Hessian hospital ship *Sally*. The English hospital ship, *Lion*, had rammed the *Swan* during the night, making the latter unfit for use. A passing transport ship, *Lucretia*, gave us the wished-for report that the 51 ships missing from the fleet, were again safe with a ship-of-the-line. The news was the more pleasant for us because we had worried about those ships, and had been unable to learn anything of their fate until now. Today the weather was rather pleasant and as warm as in summer in Hesse. According to today's observation, we were at 31°38' north latitude. During the afternoon, the wind began to blow very strongly, and changed to a storm toward evening. We began to have a scarcity of provisions, and had almost nothing but the ship's provisions, because most of our provisions had been lost in the storm.

The 20th of January - Last night was the worst that we have yet had. The storm raged until noon today, without letup. The ship received such strong jolts from the waves that everyone felt it could not stand this force much longer without sustaining damage. According to the reckoning of the crew, we were driven back a great distance last night, and to our collective displeasure, the contrary wind continued to blow.

The 21st of January - We had rainy weather, but it was also warm and pleasant, and the wind was favorable. Suddenly, during the afternoon, there was a whirlwind, which tore the fore topsail of a ship traveling near us. The ship immediately raised the distress flag, because we were far behind [the fleet]. No warship was nearby and the weather was foggy. Toward evening, the ship in distress was far behind.

The 22nd - The weather was pleasant and the wind favorable. According to the noon observation, we were at 32°38' north latitude. During the afternoon, three of the missing ships returned. We still know nothing of the others.

The 24th of January - At daybreak a three-masted ship was seen in the distance. Two warships of our fleet chased and overtook it. However, it was not an enemy, but an English merchant ship coming from the West Indies. The warships had captured an enemy schooner last night. We had rainy weather all day, and the wind blew from the west, completely contrary. The sea was calm.

The 25th of January - The weather was cold and unpleasant. By today's observation, we were at 32°12', and the ship's captain said we were fifty leagues from land. Note - Twenty leagues make one degree. The wind remained contrary. Today the ship's provisions, which were for seventy days, were cut in half.

The 26th - Today we had the same weather as yesterday, but the wind was favorable for us, and rather strong from the northeast. During the afternoon, the wind swung back and was from the northwest. A great many fish appeared on the surface of the sea, and the weather began to grow stormy again.

The 27th of January - Due to last night's stormy weather and a strong contrary wind, we were again driven far from land. According to the noon observation, we were at 32°39' north latitude. At noon the wind veered to the northwest and toward evening, to the southwest. Today we had the coldest weather since leaving New York. The warship signaled that it had found bottom with the lead line. Later, the warship and several others changed the signal to mean they had seen land. Many seagulls, which seldom go far from land, are flying about us and support the signal. We waited impatiently to see the foothills, but saw none today. A large turtle swam past our ship. We are no longer sorry that we could not catch it.

The 28th of January - The stormy weather, during the past night, caused us to be struck hard by the waves, which distressed us even more because we believed we were near to land, and there are a great many hidden sandbanks in this region. Today was somewhat more peaceful and pleasant. We had favorable wind until noon, and were at 32°51' north latitude. After several attempts, we found a sandy bottom at twenty fathoms. Today we saw many ducks and gulls. During the afternoon, the wind swung to the northwest, and we had to sail away from the land. Sunset gave us a most pleasant scene today, which this magnificent orb of day had never before offered us. Before the lower part of the circle, as the sun set, was lost from view, and seemed almost to rest on the ocean, it appeared to our eyes as a fiery, round body resting on a fiery pyramid, which seemed to gradually sink into the sea.

<u>The 29th of January</u> - Last night the wind swung to our favor. This morning ,we sailed eight English miles in an hour, and toward noon, at six miles an hour. According to the noon observation, we were at 32°33' north latitude. The fleet has never risked using so many sails as on this day, and as can only be unfurled, with such a full wind. We found bottom at fourteen and fifteen fathoms. Our ship's captain discovered land lying at a distance of five or six leagues, from the top of the mainmast, at three o'clock in the afternoon. About four o'clock in the afternoon, we encountered the remaining warships from our fleet. The fleet lay to until these warships had joined us, and the fleet had assembled near one another. We assume that they, [the warships] must have already escorted the missing part of the fleet into the Savannah River. Toward evening, the transport ship *Eliza*, on which were Captains Bode and Neumann, to our great joy, drew near our ship, and we learned that they were all still well. We had not seen this ship since Sandy Hook, and were therefore all the more concerned, as we had reason to doubt it was in fit condition to stay out of danger, which we now heard was the case.

<u>The 30th of January</u> - Last night the fleet lay to before the wind. This morning there was no wind, and toward noon it sprang up, but as it was contrary, we

had to tack. At noon today we were at 31°32' north latitude. Toward evening the wind swung to our favor, and from the top of the mainmast, land could be seen. Because the land in this region is very low, it can not be seen at a great distance, but only when one approaches near to it.

The 31st of January - Today we enjoyed a pleasant day such as we have never in memory had at sea before. Although the sun shone brightly all day, it was so foggy all around us, that our horizon was not more than an English mile, and the entire fleet could never be seen. This was the reason we could not find the entrance to the Savannah River, nor even see the land. In the fog, the admiral and part of the fleet had become separated from us, and to prevent losing the fleet, he fired cannon shots steadily, so that we could steer accordingly. The warship with us answered the cannon shots. At noon we were at 31°52' north latitude. At four o'clock in the afternoon, we lay at anchor, although the entire fleet had still not assembled.

The 1st of February - About ten o'clock this morning, the *Romulus*, which was the only warship with us, weighed anchor, and all the transport and store ships, of which there were 36, followed. We sailed back into the sea. According to the noon observation, we were at 31°51' north latitude. As soon as we reached the open sea, we set our course straight for land. Toward four o'clock in the afternoon, we saw seven of the warships belonging to our fleet, at anchor. When we reached them, we discovered for the first time, to our great joy, that we could see land directly ahead of us, from the deck. The weather today was like yesterday.

The 2nd of February - Toward noon, the warships *Romulus* and *Roebuck* weighed anchor. The transport ships lying nearby did likewise and steered toward the land lying ahead of us. At five o'clock in the afternoon, we were lying at anchor in the mouth of the Savannah River, near the lighthouse on Tybee Island, seventeen English miles from Savannah. A large number of ships were already lying here. The transport ship *Polly*, with two grenadier companies of the Linsing Grenadier Battalion had already arrived here three weeks previously. The two companies camped on Tybee Island, as had Major [Melchior] Martini and his company of the Huyn Regiment.

The 3rd of February - Last night, despite being at anchor, was very restless for us. We could not picture the danger, and we could not even have called it a danger. With the outgoing tide, our ship grounded with such a load crash that everyone was alarmed and went on deck. No one wanted to remain below deck, fearing the ship would breakup, but because the entire fleet lay at anchor all about us, we thought about the boats and lost our fear. With the flood tide the ship floated free. We had to raise the anchor at once and tack until morning. We sailed three times toward land before taking a pilot on board at seven o'clock in the morning. He took us to a safe place. We landed today on Tybee Island. From the lighthouse, which is built of bricks and has 216 steps leading to the upper level, there is a splendid view of the surrounding area. A man lives inside in order to make a signal for ships entering [the harbor], and he is the only resident on the island. The ruins of destroyed homes, of which there were three, and which had been destroyed by the French last fall, were still visible. The entire island was wild and underdeveloped, and cut up everywhere by salt creeks coming from the ocean. As it was very flat and completely level, these creeks ran onto the land at high tide, and made all the soil salty. Nothing but tall salt grass grew there. There were also horses and pigs on the island, but very wild, not due to nature, but to the many snares which they have suffered. The jaegers had shot some raccoons. Many traces of alligators or crocodiles were evident. Supposedly there are many crocodiles in the Savannah River. We encountered many wild doves here, which were somewhat larger than a turtle dove. A type of woodpecker was nearly as large as a medium-size hen, and had a black color with a red band around the neck. This bird had very strong tail feathers which were as sharp as needles at the outer end. When it climbs a tree, it holds to the tree each time with these points. Many so-called Virginia nightingales (or rice, or Carolina birds) were seen on this island. A type of bird of prey, which is as large, and resembles a Welsh hen, and completely black, is seen here in large numbers. They are called turkey buzzards. In peace time, there is a law here against shooting them, because they eat snakes and other vermin. The creeks were full of oysters.

There are many wild laurel trees which bear fruit, as well as a great number of turpentine trees. The cabbage palmetto, or cabbage tree, grows everywhere. A great many of these were chopped down by the soldiers. The hearts were taken out and eaten. This tree grows in the shape of a willow, the branches of which fall outward, although the trunk of the tree is somewhat taller. At the top, where the willow has a crown, the cabbage palmetto has a crown also. From the tree, or from the top, very long leaves grow like broad reeds in a pond, but otherwise there are no branches. The heart [or edible part] sits at the top of the tree and is in proportion to the thickness of the trunk. In many I have seen the heart nearly as thick as the thickness of the human leg. At the tip, the heart is sort of soft, and toward the root, gradually gets harder and inedible. It can be eaten raw or cooked. When cooked, it tastes nearly like a potato; raw, it tastes like a Welsh or turkey nut. Under the shell, or rind, the tree has coarse red hair. It does not burn in fire, or at least, only after aging a long time. Because it is soft, supposedly a cannonball can not pierce it, but the wood only gives. I can not say whether this is true. We find a great many felled trees, which the French chopped down last fall, in order to take them to Savannah for the construction of wooden redoubts. Later, they sought to burn them, but they were undamaged by the fire.

A shrub which grows no taller than a man, and which has leaves growing at the bottom similar to those of a palmetto, the difference being that they are not as long, but are sharp as a needle on the end, are in great numbers. They shot up to a point at the top. A kind of grape is found on it, which fruit, about as large as a middle-size pickle, hangs from the stem, with about eight or ten such fruit on the stem. Inside they appear dark violet and taste sweet. Our captain assured us that it was the fruit described by [Captain James] Cook, during his travels, as wild bananas. We can not learn the name of many other bushes and various other trees, because the island is not inhabited. On almost all trees a great amount of long moss grows, which hangs down almost a yard. It has black hair within, almost as long as the moss. Horses, cattle, and sheep like to eat it, and much prefer it to the miserable salt grass. This moss is dried, and then the hair is separated and cleaned. It then serves the same purposes as horse hair. Water, fresh water, is not to be found on the island. However, near the lighthouse there is a miserable little spring, which provides barely enough for the man living there. Therefore, we had to arrange today for the empty water kegs to be sent to Savannah, and refilled there.

<u>The 9th of February</u> - Although many ships were still missing, and the fleet was not fully assembled here, which caused us to fear that they may have been scattered or sunk during the storm, we set sail today after provisions and water were provided for thirty days. Toward evening, the warships *Europa* and *Russell*, which had been cruising in the meantime, joined us, and we then lay at anchor. A part of the fleet remained lying at Tybee Island, but no ships with troops on board.

The 10th of February - With a good and favorable wind we slowly sailed up the coast. We could see it to the west at all times. Today's trip was exceptionally pleasant.

The 11th of February - As we approached too near to the land last night, we found it necessary to anchor. We saw land very near to us to the west and north. The anchor was raised about eight o'clock this morning, and the fleet, which now consisted of 47 transport ships and a row galley, because the warships could not advance so close to the land, but had to remain in the ocean, entered the North Edisto River at noon, and lay at anchor near the mouth of the river, between the islands. At four o'clock in the afternoon, the Jaegers, Light Infantry, and British and Hessian Grenadiers landed on Simon's Island, and marched to Simon's house the same evening. It was believed that a bridge there led across a creek to John's Island.

The 12th of February - The rest of the troops, except for the Artillery which had to remain on board the ships because of a shortage of horses, landed on the previously mentioned island, and immediately marched to join the troops which landed yesterday. All the troops carried provisions from the ships for three days, and marched to John's Island yet today.

The transport ships remained lying in the North Edisto River, and all their boats were landed with provisions today, and sent to the army along the various creeks which create these islands.

The 13th of February - The army marched in a column along the road to Charleston, as far as the Williams' House. The Huyn Regiment remained at the place where the previous camp had been, and a company of the regiment was detached to Simon's Island, where the troops had landed.

The 16th of February - The corps marched to the meeting house and lay in bivouac there, because we had not brought tents with us from New York.

The 21st of February - The Hessian Grenadier Brigade entered camp near Tanning's House.

The 25th of February - Near Hamilton's House, a part of the troops were transferred across from John's Island to James' Island. The Jaegers, 33rd and 7th Regiments remained on the first island near Stono Ferry. This was to prevent the enemy cutting off the supplies from the transport ships lying in the North Edisto River. We, on the Stono River, which divides John's and James' Islands from one another, had communications [with the transports]. The 63rd and

64th Regiments remained near Tanning's House. The grenadiers entered camp near Hamilton's House, close to the Stono River, where they had landed. John's Island is a beautiful, level island, with very beautiful plantations, which produce rice, indigo, and a sort of cotton, which grows on a bush. Tobacco is also produced. A large number of turpentine trees, which make up most of the forests, grow there. The roads are almost always long, narrow alleys created by these very tall turpentine trees. The soil is sandy. Everywhere we saw the ruins of huts in which troops commanded by General Prevost lived last year on this island. Signs were to be seen in every house that the inhabitants had been treated as enemies by these troops. The plundering must have been very extensive.

The 27th of February - A number of transport ships arrived in the North Edisto River from Tybee Island, and lay to near the fleet already there. The two grenadier companies of the 63rd and 64th Regiments were on these ships, which had become separated from our fleet, and until now, were believed to have been lost. There was also one battalion of the 71st Regiment of Highlanders, which came from Savannah, and two companies of Negroes. The others were store ships and horse ships, the latter from Savannah, with a number of wagons. These ships brought news that the warship *Defiance*, 64 guns, of our fleet, had stranded in the Savannah River.

The 28th of February - After the troops and horses, which arrived yesterday in the North Edisto River, marched to the army, the cannons and artillery from the transport ships were taken in boats on the water to James' Island. Because the horses brought with them were insufficient to pull them, horses were taken from all the officers, and all the captured horses were used to pull the artillery and wagons.

The 28th [sic] - The Hessian grenadier battalions marched to Fort Johnston, which covered the entrance to Charleston Harbor, and entered camp there. As soon as this was discovered by the enemy, ships lying in the harbor, two frigates, moved before the position and began a heavy bombardment. A grenadier of the field watch of the Graf Grenadier Battalion was killed, and one wounded in the arm. The camp had to be moved back as quickly as possible, because it was in their field of fire. Charleston lay opposite us, on the left wing, where the river is about four miles wide. The ruins of Fort Johnston, which General Prevost destroyed last year, could still be seen. It had been built of brick, oyster shells, and palmetto logs. Opposite lay Fort Moultrie, on Sullivan's Island, which is strongly fortified, and is occupied by the enemy. Between the forts lie four large, enemy frigates and a number of other armed craft at the entrance to the harbor, which is about two miles wide at this point. Many more ships lie near Charleston.

The 10th of March - Nothing of interest has occurred since the previous date, except that on 4 March, the Artillery arrived and was landed near the headquarters, which is at Hick's House, nine miles to our rear. Due to a shortage of horses, it remained there. As we needed cannons here in the meantime, the grenadiers had to pull them here, and carry the ammunition also. A redoubt was constructed in an old churchyard behind Fort Johnston, and cannons and ammunition were delivered. Because many dead bodies were dug up in the churchyard, which arouse our curiosity as this island was not heavily populated, we asked the reason, and were told they were soldiers from only two English regiments, which had been stationed in barracks in the area. Both regiments had nearly died out within a year of their arrival here. This report caused us to wish that we will not remain here for any prolonged period. All the troops have now assembled on this island. Today the Light Infantry, British grenadiers, and the 7th, 23rd, and 33rd Regiments crossed over to the other side of the Wappoo Creek on the [newly] built bridge, and established posts on the Ashley River, opposite Charleston, on Wappoo Neck. The Jaegers also crossed. These troops began to throw up batteries opposite the city. Two French frigates, some brigantines, a rebel frigate, and several row galleys came from the city, and lay under Fort Moultrie. Our warships, of which ten or twelve could be counted in the distance, lay just outside the bar, and had blockaded the harbor. Today both the Linsing and Lengercke Grenadier Battalions marched to the place where the English grenadiers and Light Infantry stood. The enemy ships delivered a heavy fire of grape shot against our command in Fort Moultrie today, but it had not the least effect.

The 11th of March - Two frigates from England joined Admiral Arbuthnot outside the bar. Twenty-three much needed provisions ships, which came with them, sailed to Tybee Island. Majors Balfour and Fuchs arrived from England in the frigates.

The 12th of March - The batteries at Wappoo Neck, mentioned on the tenth of the month, fired against the city for the first time.

The 13th of March - Last night, thirty days' provisions were delivered to the redoubt by our camp. A detachment of 120 men of Major General von Huyn's Brigade relieved the grenadiers on duty there.

The 17th of March - The Vacant and Graf Grenadier Battalions marched to join the two other battalions at their headquarters near the Hick's House.

The 18th, 19th, and 20th of March - Our warships crossed the bar. Our transport ships, which had been in the North Edisto River, came from there through the Stono Inlet and up the Stono River, and lay near the headquarters at Hick's House. Here, where previously nothing larger than two-masted vessels had lain, were to be seen a great fleet of large ships.

The 21st of March - Most of the enemy ships which had lain near Fort Moultrie moved closer to Charleston, which lies about six English miles from the fort.

The 22nd of March - The three grenadier battalions, Linsing, Lengercke, and Vacant, marched across the Wappoo Creek, and occupied the camp of the English and the Jaegers, who had gone inland beyond Randolph's Bridge today.

The 24th of March - The Graf Grenadier Battalion also crossed Wappoo Creek and occupied the place of the Linsing Grenadier Battalion, which had moved forward to Randolph's Bridge today.

The 27th of March - Ninety flatboats and long boats came up the Wappoo Creek and lay at Wappoo Neck under the cover of a battery of six 32-pound cannons, opposite Charleston, to the southeast.

The 28th of March - Last night, the flatboats and long boats, noted yesterday, went out of Wappoo Creek, escorted by two cannon boats, and went about four miles up Ashley River. They had to pass close to the enemy cannons. They lay hidden all day in a small creek behind our camp. At one o'clock in the afternoon the troops moved out, and marched in the following order, which the enemy in the city could observe: two battalions of British grenadiers, the vacant Minnigerode Grenadier Battalion, Graf Grenadier Battalion, Lengercke Grenadier Battalion, 7th and 23rd Regiments, and at Randolph's Bridge, which we crossed today, General Paterson joined us, having come from Savannah by land. The 2nd Battalion of the 71st Regiment of this corps joined with us. The rest of the mentioned corps, however, marched to our former camp on Wappoo Neck, while the Linsing Grenadier Battalion, two battalions of light infantry, and the 33rd Regiment and the Hessian Jaegers joined us. We bivouacked in a woods not far from Drayton's Ferry. Major General von Huyn's Brigade had remained, part at James' Island and part at Wappoo Neck, in order to cover our transport and provision ships. Also, all our baggage, except for the little we had with us, lay at the latter place.

The 29th of March - The little baggage, and the horses, which we had with us, were taken to Ashley

Ferry to be carried across. At daybreak the troops began their march to Drayton's Ferry, and were taken across the Ashley River in the following order, using the flatboats and long boats which had gone up the Ashley River last night: the Hessian Jaegers with two cannon boats were the advance guard, two battalions of light infantry, two battalions of British grenadiers, the four Hessian grenadier battalions, the 7th, 23rd, and 33rd Regiments, and the 2nd Battalion of the 71st Regiment. The enemy assembled on the northwest bank of the Ashley River, took flight immediately, without making the least resistance. The troop crossing with the regimental artillery was accomplished in the shortest possible time, considering we had nothing but regimental artillery with us. The senior agent for the fleet, Master Tomkins, supervised the project and, as with every such opportunity, displayed his outstanding abilities as well as accomplishing his daily activities. As soon as everyone was across, the troops marched in a column in the above order toward Charleston. The boats returned to Ashley Ferry, the troops entered camp, here, and the baggage and horses were brought over.

The 30th of March - As soon as all the horses and baggage had joined us from Ashley Ferry this morning, the army moved out, and at the same time, the boats sailed from the mentioned place back down the river. The troops marched directly toward Charleston, on the main road, in a column. Some miles short of the enemy lines, the Jaegers began to exchange fire with the enemy. About two or three miles from the city, Lord Keitney, adjutant general to the commander-in-chief, [probably Earl Cathcart] was wounded. The Jaegers and Light Infantry pressed close to the enemy lines. The fire between the outposts continued until late at night, without effect. The army bivouacked about two or three miles from Charleston, in an arch which extended from the Ashley River to the Cooper River. The boats, which had gone from Ashley Ferry down to Wappoo Creek today, began bringing siege equipment across to Charleston Neck this evening.

The 31st of March - The project of [bringing over] siege equipment continued all day. The enemy fired cannon at the outposts without effect. At night, a large detachment of 1,500 men was sent to work on the trenches.

The 1st of April - The work detachment sent out last night, completed nearly three trenches. Because the soil is sandy, the work went quickly. Walls made of planks were already at Wappoo Neck for this purpose. They were covered with sand on both sides, which greatly simplified the work. The cannon fire from the enemy, day and night, was without effect. Many small vessels went from the city up the Cooper River, which made us think the inhabitants were taking their families and belongings inland.

The 2nd of April - A detachment, equally as strong as that of last night, moved out. All day long boats went to the city, and again, inland on the Cooper River.

The 3rd of April - Everything was the same as yesterday.

The 4th of April - The enemy threw bombs from the city against our batteries, and did so strongly. A ship in the Cooper River flanked our troops in the trenches, and forced them to withdraw. Seven bombs fell into one of our redoubts, but without effect, except to kill one English grenadier, and wound one other. There were still no cannons in our new batteries. The work continued during the night.

The 5th of April - The enemy continued to harass our workers with a continuous cannon fire, but without effect. Today an English officer was wounded and two grenadiers killed. From seven o'clock yesterday morning, until seven o'clock today, the enemy fired 573 heavy cannonballs at us.

The 6th of April - Everything continued as yesterday.

The 7th of April - Ten schooners came down the Cooper River with a 1,000 man reinforcement under the command, on board, of General [Charles] Scott. They had marched from Stony Point on the North River in New Jersey last December, and had been almost four months on this difficult march. As soon as they arrived at Charleston, which occurred at sundown, a loud cheer was heard in the city, with a continuous ringing of all the bells.

The 8th of April - We had one of the most beautiful scenes. At four o'clock in the afternoon, nine of our warships passed Fort Moultrie on the flood tide, by dull weather, and a strong south wind. The firing on both sides was exceptionally heavy. The tenth ship ran upon a sandbank near the mentioned fort. The ships had to pass very close under the enemy cannons, which raked them constantly. *Roebuck* was the first ship, and *Renown* the second ship. They had their foremasts shot away, otherwise there was no damage to the others. *Romulus* lay to opposite the fort and fired a continuous bombardment. Despite the strong wind, nothing could be seen of the ships but the flashes, due to the smoke. The majesty of this sight can hardly be described. As soon as the ships had all passed Fort Moultrie, the general excitement in the city could be felt, because all the cannons and mortars grew quiet. Nearly 6,000 men were on the wall, who wanted the pleasure of seeing the ships blown out of the water. As soon as the second [ship] cleared the fire from the fort, everyone left the wall, and shortly thereafter, a great many small vessels were seen on the Cooper River, heading inland. This and the road to Mount Pleasant were the only communications which the city had with the interior. The city was now completely cut off. We therefore had revenge for yesterday's cheering. The rebel and French ships retreated, part into the Cooper River, part under the city's defenses, and made not the least effort to move. The enemy had sunk many ships so that ours could not approach too near the city, and be in a position to fire against them. Our ships had seven dead and fifteen wounded. The large ships could not cross over the bar, but had to remain in the ocean. *Renown*, 50 guns, was the largest that could cross.

The 9th of April - We received news that the tenth ship, which ran aground yesterday, was a transport ship, and last night, because it could not be floated free, it was set on fire. Today four cannon boats and two flatboats equipped with cannons, were brought here, overland, about two English miles, from the Ashley River to the Cooper River, on a locally built machine which had two wheels in the front and a skid behind. The machine was pulled by the Negroes. The enemy were very busy moving their belongings out of the city and into the country, on the Cooper River.

The 10th of April - Our seventh redoubt was completed tonight, and so near the enemy lines that it was possible to fire a rifle into the enemy lines from the trenches. For this purpose a detachment of jaegers was sent forward. Three enemy frigates, which lay in the Cooper River, in order to outflank our works, returned to the city today.

The 11th of April - Several Englanders were wounded, among others the adjutant general for Lord Cornwallis, named Viceroy. The work and guard detachments were provided as noted above. They consisted of a general, three staff officers, fifteen captains, and 1,500 men. A ship with cannons and ammunitions, such as had brought us from New York, had sunk. The artillerymen who had been on it, were rescued and taken to Bermuda, which created a great problem for us. This situation was also the reason that the siege could not be started earlier. Of a necessity, also, cannons had to be taken out of the large warships, and then brought here on land. The shortage of artillerymen was made good with sailors.

The 12th of April - Three small vessels passed Fort Moultrie, and were fired on, heavily, but without effect. Supposedly these are meant to cut off the enemy's route to Mount Pleasant, which lies north of Charleston. The cannon fire and throwing of bombs into our lines by the enemy was stronger than usual today.

The 13th of April - At ten o'clock this morning our batteries opened fire, heavily and in earnest, on the city, and the enemy returned the fire with an equal strength. It continued uninterrupted until eight o'clock in the evening. Today, firebombs were also fired into the city, setting fire to the governor's and commandant's houses, as soon as the use of these bombs began. The Hessian Artillery shot the fire bombs. The enemy works suffered great damage today, and several of their cannons were dismounted. One of our batteries also suffered severely.

The 14th of April - Cannon fire from both sides

was heavy. Today we received the news that [Sir William] Shaw, Earl Cathcart's Legion, and Ferguson's Corps attacked a rebel corps thirty miles from here, between the Cooper and Ashley Rivers, capturing 100 prisoners, including three officers, and nearly as many horses. Seven men were cut down on the spot. Toward evening, two cannon boats passed the enemy ships in the Cooper River and, near Mount Pleasant, captured a boat, whose crew abandoned it upon the approach of our boats. A three-masted ship was then attacked, but did not reply to the cannon fire directed against it. However, a battery and an armed ship on the Wandow River did reply, forcing the cannon boats to retire.

The 16th of April - A ship loaded with ammunition arrived from St. Augustine in Florida. It brought an 18-inch mortar. A ship also arrived today from Savannah with ammunition and cannons, among which were several pieces taken from the French during the siege of Savannah. Today the prisoners captured by the Cathcart Legion arrived, as well as 24 four-horse wagons and 315 horses. This afternoon a row galley took position in the Cooper River, on our flank. This forced the 7th Regiment to leave its camp. The fire was delivered mostly against the houses in which the English hospital had been established. During the evening, heavy cannons were brought up, which forced the row galley to leave the position. This could not have been accomplished by the English metal 6-pounders, nor the Hessian field pieces. The latter fire nearly as far as the English 6-pounders.

The 17th of April - An enemy frigate sailed up the Cooper River, supposedly either to prevent Colonel [James] Webster, of the 33rd Regiment, who had gone inland with a small corps, from crossing the river, or, if he had already crossed, as is reported, to cut his communications.

The 30th of April - Since the last date the work has gone forward every night, as noted above. On our side, we were now approaching so close to the enemy that it was possible to throw a stone into the enemy lines. A reinforcement arrived from New York, consisting of the Ditfurth Regiment, the 42nd Regiment of Scots, the Queen's Rangers, [Francis], Lord Rawdon's Corps, and Colonel Brown's Corps. The 42nd Regiment, Queen's Rangers, and Lord Rawdon's Corps joined us. The Ditfurth Regiment and Brown's Corps relieved the Huyn Regiment at Wappoo Neck, which then returned to James' Island to take the place of the 63rd Regiment covering the ships. The latter regiment joined us. After the arrival of this reinforcement, Lord Cornwallis crossed the Cooper River with a small corps, and joined Colonel Webster.

The fire of cannons and small arms, by both sides, continued day and night. Until today, the siege troops have had more than 200 dead and wounded. Four days ago, five small armed vessels sailed on the river between the city and Sullivan's Island, and through a creek behind Shute's Island, to Mount Pleasant, in order to give assistance to Lord Cornwallis' efforts to capture a small fort at that place. We heard today that the capture had taken place, and 88 men were captured. These small vessels had to withstand a heavy cannonade from Fort Moultrie. Four days ago, a part of Lord Cornwallis' Corps landed on Shute's Island, which was on our left flank, on the west side of the Cooper River, and to our great joy, raised the English flag over a fort situated on the bank of the mentioned river. The enemy had vacated the fort upon our approach. The besieged in Charleston were now cut off on all sides, on land. All ships in the Cooper River retired close to the city. The small enemy vessels in the Cooper and Wandow River, loaded with merchandise, were taken as prizes by our vessels, and immediately fitted out as privateers. By this means we were completely masters of these rivers.

The 4th of May - During the night, a three-masted ship lying near the city was silently boarded by our side, and brought away in the morning. When it was inspected, to our great surprise, we found that the only men on board were those suffering from small pox. With reference to small pox, I must take note here, that the people of this country, just as in Germany, fear it as much as the black plague. People who get it are immediately isolated. [There appears to be a portion of the German text missing at this point.] We were now in constant communication with Lord Cornwallis. A boat with enemy officers, who apparently did not want to wait for the end of the siege, was captured last night. Today the 64th Regiment returned from Lord Cornwallis' Corps, and brought us the news that Lord Cornwallis, with the rest of his corps, consisting of the 23rd and 33rd Regiments, Lord Rawdon's and Ferguson's Corps, Cathcart's Legion, and several provincial corps, had gone farther inland to the north.

The 7th of May - The investment was continued as above. Our Jaegers have done great damage to the enemy in the city. Otherwise nothing has especially affected the siege since the last entry. The sailors in one of the batteries, despite orders to the contrary not to shoot at the houses in the city, have done so, causing the greatest damage. The fire from this battery can be distinguished by an unceasing persistence, and these jacks [sailors] often fire a full broadside. Today, we learned in orders, that Lieutenant Asch, of the mounted British Light Infantry, had been captured by the enemy, but was then rescued by Colonel [Banastre] Tarleton. Colonel Tarleton cut down more than twenty men, and captured 36 men and 100 horses.

Colonel [William] Washington and [Anthony] White, and most of the rest [of the Americans] supposedly were caught on the river and the swamp near Hell Hole, and drowned as they sought to save themselves by flight. We were also informed by the orders that the British flag had been raised over Fort Moultrie on Sullivan's Island, but have heard no further particulars regarding the capture.

The 8th of May - We learned that Captain [Sir Andrew Snape] Hammond, of the navy, with sailors and marines, had attacked and captured Fort Moultrie. A large part of the defenders had already withdrawn, and only 184 men were captured. However, they had provisions for 500 men for six months. Forty-one large cannons and a 10-inch mortar were also found therein. The fort reportedly was oblong and very strong. It is built of palmetto logs and lies parallel with the ships' cannons. Of the enemy ships, all but five three-masted ships, near the city, have been sunk, although there are still a large number of very small ones. This morning the enemy was called upon to surrender, and therefore there was a ceasefire. The cannonade was very heavy through the past night.

The 9th of May - The ceasefire lasted until nine o'clock this evening, but because the city would not surrender according to offered articles, the cannonade and bombardment was resumed in earnest by both sides. Our closest parallel extended to the canal connecting the Cooper and Ashley Rivers, and small arms fire could be directed into the enemy embrasures. Therefore, kegs of musket cartridges were placed in the trenches so that the troops could fire at will.

The 10th of May - Last night Lieutenant [Johann Jakob] Fritsch, of our battalion, was severely wounded in the head. The cannon fire, as well as small arms fire, continued very heavy day and night. However, the enemy fire began to slacken, but our side fired all the more steadily.

The 11th of May - The enemy sent a flag of truce from the city asking for a ceasefire, as they were ready to negotiate a surrender.

The 12th of May - Following an agreement yesterday to capitulate, the troops of the garrison marched out of Charleston through the Hornwork this morning at ten-thirty with music playing and flags flying. As they were not allowed to play a British march, they chose a Turkish one. Near the Hornwork the prisoners stacked their arms. The number of Continentals and militia, including officers, amounts to 6,000 men. Seven generals, 1 commodore, 10 regular regiments and 3 battalions of artillery, not counting the French nor militia men, were captured. General Leslie took possession of the city and the defensive works facing our lines, with the grenadier companies of the 7th and Guards Regiments, and four cannons. As soon as this had taken place and the enemy flag lowered and the British flag raised, the 7th and 63rd Regiments marched into the city. Meantime, all of our troops entered the lines. The militia was not allowed to march out with the others, and their weapons were taken from them in the city. This applied to the French, also. Officers were permitted to keep their swords. After the captives had surrendered their weapons, they were returned to the city during the afternoon. The number of cannons in the defenses, including metal ones, supposedly amounts to 400. The ammunition magazines are considerable, but provisions, except for a few items, had been nearly exhausted, which is said to have been the primary reason the city had to surrender. During the entire siege, our troops suffered 205 dead and wounded. The

Graf Grenadier Battalion had two officers, Lieutenants Fritsch and [Andreas] Oelhans, wounded, and two grenadiers killed and eight wounded.

The 13th, 14th, and 15th of May - The militia prisoners were released to their homes, inland, on parole. Today, a powder magazine, in which there was a great amount of munitions, blew up, without anyone knowing the cause initially. Although uncertain, it was said the enemy weapons were taken there, one had fired (accidentally), and this had caused the disaster. The number of victims can not be learned with certainty, but could amount to several hundred. Of the Hessians, an artilleryman, a cannoneer, and a carpenter, both of the Linsing Grenadier Battalion, were killed. This afternoon the Dirfurth and Huyn Regiments crossed the Ashley River from Wappoo Neck, and entered quarters in the city. The 42nd Regiment also moved in.

The 21st of May - Nothing of consequence has happened since the last entry, except the officers' side arms were taken away because they created disorders in the city. Hoards of militia went past our camp, and inland, our transport ships exited the Stono River, crossed the bar, and entered the Charleston Harbor. We received orders to be prepared to embark on designated ships which brought us from New York, and on which our baggage was still being held. Meanwhile, a number of Negroes, who had followed and taken employment with the army, part due to the shortage of foodstuffs, part to get away from their masters, began demolishing the defensive positions erected by us against the city. The corps designated for embarkation were the Jaegers, Light Infantry, British and Hessian Grenadiers, the 42nd Regiment, and the Queen's Rangers

The 22nd of May - The Jaegers, two British grenadier battalions, and the Linsing, Lengercke, and vacant Minnigerode Grenadier Battalion marched to Ashley Ferry. The Graf Grenadier Battalion remained in its old camp.

The 27th and 28th of May - The above listed troops returned, and entered their former camps.

The 29th of May - The Light Infantry returned, also.

The 30th of May - The Jaegers embarked in their formerly assigned ships in the Cooper River.

The 31st of May - The British and Hessian Grenadiers embarked. In compliance with today's general orders, each regiment was allowed to take ten

Negroes, whose masters were in rebel service.

The 1st of June - The rest of the troops assigned to the expedition were embarked. It is said that these troops are embarked for Wilmington, in North Carolina.

The 4th of June - The ships sailed away from the city. Today we passed Fort Moultrie, whose breastworks were made of palmetto logs, which were laid out in a square, one on top of the other, and filled with oyster shells. We could not cross the bar today. Many ships run aground here. The warships had crossed the bar already yesterday and lay at anchor outside. This difficult expedition, during which the Graf Grenadier Battalion, as noted, suffered one seriously wounded and one lightly wounded officer, two grenadiers dead and eight wounded, and one grenadier captured, therefore came to an end. The number of sick was tolerable, considering the difficult sea voyage, the subsequent duty, and the poor living conditions in an unhealthy climate, where the troops continuously had to lie under the open sky. Although the heat was very oppressive during the day, it changed, as soon as the sunset, to a cold, penetrating fog, which made everything damp and wet. It grew steadily colder as night set in, and by early morning had turned to ice. The land itself is full of swamps and morasses. For the most part, the water is bad and in the shallow well sand springs, it is warm as milk, or even hotter, all day long. In the deeper wells, it is colder, but after standing for a short time in a barrel, it is warm enough for a bath. Vegetables and garden produce are surprisingly rare. Therefore it would not have been surprising if we had had more sickness than we actually had.

Charleston is about four or five English miles in circumference. I could not learn the exact number of houses, as many were burned down during last fall and this spring, but there were many beautiful ones and some were really splendid. The same can be said for the rural area. The streets are laid out quite straight. In proportion to the surrounding area, Charleston could have more houses as there are many gardens there, and also a great many large open areas. In addition, for the most part, the houses are built at a distance from one another, so that air can circulate from all sides of the streets. Due to a shortage of stones, most of the streets are not paved, unfortunately, and on the sides of the houses there are only narrow footpaths for the pedestrians, which are often impassable. In the middle of the street the sand is ground fine. This is driven by the wind, and causes discomfort for the eyes. This devil is excepted by the people in the front rooms of their houses because they are accustomed to keeping the windows open at all times, due to the great heat. The city is surrounded with defensive positions. The fortifications are still made with palmetto logs, as noted in the above description of Fort Moultrie. All European nationalities are encountered in Charleston. The German Jews have noticeably multiplied, and large numbers of Germans live here, who still speak as pure a German as any that I have heard in America.

Commerce in Charleston is important, as noted by the products shipped out. Presently there is little trace of that, because most of the people and the leading citizens have not yet returned.

The inhabitants are whites and blacks, although the number of the latter exceeds the first. The first, for the most part, have a pale yellow appearance. The males, especially in the country, are thin and rather tall, and generally taller than Europeans. I can not praise the beauty of the females as they are also pale yellow, and very few that I have met, have a fresh complexion. Still, most of these had fled inland, also. Both sexes are lazy and not capable of working. This is left to the Ethiopians. I have not seen the whites engaged in any work except trade. Everything is done by the Negroes, who are in every house in great numbers, and often even more than are necessary. Those who serve their masters in the city and on the land are well care for, but the lot of the field Negroes on the plantations is all the more strenuous, and against all humanity.

The first live either with their master in a house, or in a nearby house, serving the master's house. The latter, who work the fields, are often treated worse than oxen in Europe. They go about naked and often can barely cover their shame with an old rag.

Wretched huts, made with logs placed one over the other, in which there is neither a fireplace nor a stove, are used for their homes. Their entire furnishings consist of an iron pot and some gourds, which have been hollowed out. Occasionally I have seen a bucket therein, also. For his sustenance, a Negro receives a quart - nearly equal to a Hessen half-Maas - of Indian corn or rice. This Indian corn is ground in a hand mill fastened outside his hut, and the ground corn or rice is cooked therein. As soon as it is boiling, it is taken out and eaten. Nothing is left over, as otherwise it is insufficient for his sustenance. The bed of these wretched creatures is in the ashes around the fire. These are all the means of sustenance provided, except for water. They seem to have no more intelligence than the cattle. On many plantations there are 400 to 500, or even more of these poor human beings, and the number is governed by the size of the plantation. They must work naked in the fields in the greatest heat.

Punishments are barbarous, and against all humanity for the smallest common error, and they are raised in the air with both hands tied, and whipped soundly on the bare back. For more serious infractions, a nail is fastened on the whip, and still worse crimes are punished with the most terrible cruelties. I have been told that occasionally they are whipped in the above manner till the flesh is cut from the back, and the wounds are sprinkled with salt and pepper. Sometimes the victim of such an atrocity is bound hand and foot to a tree, and allowed to be bitten nearly to death by the mosquitoes (which are called Schnaken in Germany). Many who are so punished, give up the ghost. If a master kills a Negro slave, nothing is made of it. If a Negro kills a white man, or merely raises his hand against him, there is no question, he must die. This is true, as in every case of murder by a Negro against the law, but there is seldom a case where the transgressor would be punished [if white]. Certainly necessity has caused the Negroes to be treated so harshly, not only in his style of living, but also in the manner of punishment being administered. The whites are greatly outnumbered by the blacks, who must be held down by a constant fear of the whites, otherwise they would be like unmanageable cattle. Their vindictiveness has no limits. Among themselves they speak the Guinean language, and most field Negroes understand absolutely no English. I have been told, one such Negro, raising indigo, can earn his master 500 livre per year.

In addition to indigo, the land also produces rice and a type of cotton which grows on a bush. This bush must be planted again each year. The cotton is not as good, however, as that which grows on a tree. Indian corn or Welsh corn is grown in large quantities. A sort of small pea and a gray bean, which latter item tastes like lintel, grows abundantly here, and serves as food for livestock and people. Tobacco is also grown here, but not a large quantity. In addition, this province produces most all garden products, which, however, are not comparable as to taste and size with those of the northern provinces. Many of the latter yield two crops a year. Fruit bearing trees are the peach, mulberry, and fig. I have seen nuts of various sorts and chestnuts here, as well as various kinds of grapevines. The latter ripen in July. The mulberry, black as well as white, we can eat in early May. I have seen other fruit trees in various gardens, but these were not identified, were very small, and bore no fruit. Farther inland, fruits are grown, also. Pomegranate and orange trees were found in every garden. There were entire avenues lined with waxtrees. In addition, many and various types of trees and plants are seen, from which the inhabitants do not know the names. The most pleasant of these are the turpentine trees, the evergreen oak, and the bay tree, which has a flower as large as a man's two hands placed together. The flower is oval and white as a lily. It has a very strong and pleasant aroma, and is similar to mahogany, and differentiates itself from this only by its lightness. Red and white cedars grow everywhere, also the red and white oak, and the linden. Many China trees [azaleas] are seen growing in the forests. They generally grow like a grapevine, on other trees, very tall and high up, and the roots look like potatoes or earth apples under the ground. The China [berry] is used as medicine, but is not nearly as good as that grown near the Equator, and therefore is seldom used. Sassafras also grows as abundantly here as in the northern provinces. I could not learn the names of many other trees and plants.

There are very beautifully laid out gardens in this province, which were all the more pleasing, as that is unusual in America. There is a great surplus of horses, cattle, sheep, pigs, and fowls in the southern provinces. The plantation owners themselves do not know how many they own, because many of the cattle are wild, and live in the wilderness. When the cattle see a white person approaching in the distance, they act as the wild ones do in other lands, and try to hide in the forests. On the other hand, they are not as shy around the Negroes, and can be approached and caught. There are also deer here, wild and in parks. There are many partridge, and I have seen woodcocks of all kinds. The type, which they call gallinule, is larger than a domestic chicken. The bill is nearly a foot long. They are very difficult to shoot, however, because for the most part, they sit close to one another on the salt flats, where a man can not easily hide, and part of them are always on watch. When a hunter is seen in the distance, they give a whistle at which the entire flock take flight, rising into the air. All the birds which leave the northern provinces in winter are seen here in huge flocks, and especially a very great number of wild doves come here in the winter. In the barns on the plantations and in the rice fields a great many are to be seen.

Above all, I should note, that this province, more than any other, has a large surplus of everything necessary to support human life. However, until the present this does not approach its potential. There is work enough for many hands to find a rich and overabundant life style, if they were to settle here. The unhealthy and unpleasant climate, however, may be the reason that few whites live here, although there is room for more. Despite all the houses being built in a manner suitable for a warm climate, every white person has to anticipate that he will suffer an attack of fever every year. The person is fortunate who can escape it during some years. Carolina is favored by none of the learned faculties more than by medicine. On every street in the city, a Son of Aesculapius lives. From the number of widows, I conclude that the climate is more disadvantageous to the male constitution than the female. At least a doctor born in

Berlin, but living in Charleston supports my belief. As unhealthy as it is, still I have seen several very old people, and among others, a man of 105 years on John's Island, who had served as a sailor already during the reign of Queen Anne. Because of his age, he could no longer walk, and it required strict attention to understand what he said. His beard was longer than a grenadier's, and grew all about his mouth so that it could no longer be seen, except when he opened it to speak.

South Carolina and North Carolina appear to be the richest provinces as to their exported products. The inhabitants are the richest English colonists, which can clearly be seen in their beautiful and splendid furniture and home decorations. A house is seldom entered in which the furniture is not of mahogany, and where there is much silver service. The inhabitants are very house-proud. A number of Negroes were constantly busy washing inside, and this very much aids the cooling. All day long, and especially from nine o'clock in the morning until three o'clock in the afternoon, the heat is especially penetrating. The inhabitants, for the most part, conduct their business so as to remain indoors during this time.

[The 4th of June] - Today we weighed anchor, but due to contrary wind, could not cross the bar, where the channels through the sandbanks are very narrow, and it is impossible to pass without a favorable wind. Many of the transport ships ran aground today. The warships had crossed the bar yesterday, and lay at anchor on the other side.

The 8th of June - We had to lie on this side of the bar since the last date above, due to contrary wind. Today the wind shifted in our favor, and between eight and ten o'clock in the morning the transport ships passed fortunately over the bar. After the entire fleet had assembled around the admiral's ship, we sailed out to sea at about noon. About three o'clock in the afternoon, we saw land for the last time. We steered southeast. The fleet, including the warships, consisted of about 100 ships.

The 9th of June - At noon today we were at 32°22' north latitude. From noon onward, the weather began to grow unpleasant, and toward evening changed to a storm, which made many on board seasick.

The 10th of June - This morning the storm abated, but the ocean remained rough and high. Most of those on board were seasick. One of the warships lost the top of its middle mast last night.

The 11th of June - The voyage was exceptionally pleasant. According to the noon observation, we were at 33°08' north latitude.

The 12th of June - Again, we had very pleasant sailing. The admiral's ship, most of the warships, except for two frigates and a war sloop named *Bonnetta,* as well as the agent's ship, *John*, were missing today. Aboard those ships were not only the commander-in-chief, General Clinton, but also the senior agent, Captain Tomkins.

The 13th of June - We were at 35°26' north latitude, the weather was good, and the trip pleasant. We believe now, with certainty, that we are sailing to New York. The ships noted as missing yesterday, have not returned to the fleet yet.

The 14th of June - According to today's observation we were already at 37°30' north latitude, an indication that since yesterday we had sailed more than two degrees. We saw several large fish today which we have not previously seen. The crew said they were sperm whales. At dusk a wind calm developed, and a heavy fog, so that no ship could be seen. This necessitated a constant small arms fire.

The 15th of June - According to the noon observation, we were at 37°56' north latitude. Therefore, we had not advanced very far since noon yesterday. The wind was northeast, and not favorable for us. One ship of our fleet had dropped far behind, and was attacked by an enemy ship. The latter had to cease his attack when a warship of our fleet approached it. Today, for this time of year, we had exceptionally cold weather.

The 16th of June - According to today's observation, we were at 39°50' north latitude. During the afternoon we again had very pleasant weather, and good, but weak, wind. A war sloop ordered our captain to make as much sail as possible, as a strange fleet had been seen in the distance. From the top of the mast, our ship's captain saw eight ships together, following us with full sail. At the same time, we received the report that a French fleet of warships was on this coast. Therefore, due to discovery by our ship's captain, we were in a tight corner, because we had no other warships with us, except for the two frigates, and the war sloop mentioned above. The ship's captain said that if they were warships, they would certainly have caught up with us by tomorrow morning, and it would be difficult for even one of the transport ships to escape.

The 17th of June - Early this morning, at daybreak, the ships assumed to be enemies yesterday, made a signal that they were friends. At the same time, we saw the coast of New Jersey. According to the noon observation, we were at 40°01' north latitude today. Toward four o'clock in the afternoon, we saw the lighthouse at Sandy Hook, and the lead ships entered New York Harbor. Unexpectedly, such a heavy fog developed that we could not see Sandy Hook nor a single ship. It was necessary for us to lay to before the wind. Suddenly a strong wind sprang up and stormy weather, which caused us, in fear of grounding, to sail out to sea again.

The 18th of June - As last night's fog continued, it was necessary to continue firing and beating the drums, so that the ships would not ram one another. With a strong wind and a stormy sea, we had to tack all night. In the morning we were close to Sandy Hook, surrounded by a large number of transport ships which belonged to our fleet. At nine o'clock in the morning, we dropped anchor near Cole's Ferry on Staten Island, and again met the warships on which were the admiral and General Clinton.

The 20th of June - All the troops landed on Staten Island. Each company received a house for quarters. Lieutenant General von Knyphausen had entered the region of New Jersey with all the troops [of his command].

The 21st of June -The Graf Grenadier Battalion received orders to embark at once, and to sail to New York.

The 22nd of June - The battalion landed in New York and joined the garrison there. There were no other troops in New York, but Robinson's Corps. The citizens had to do duty in the city.

The 23rd of July - We received orders to be prepared to embark. Since the 22nd of last month we have lain peacefully in New York, where the Donop Regiment has joined us. Meantime, the rest of the troops had gone up the North River, and camped at Philipse's House. There were no other troops on this island, except the Prince Charles and Young Lossberg Regiments, at Fort Knyphausen.

The 24th of July - At six o'clock in the morning, the Graf Grenadier Battalion embarked in small vessels at New York, and went through Hellgate to Whitestone, where we embarked on the two transport ships, *Margaretha Martha* and *Woodland*. The other troops embarked here were 250 Hessian Jaegers, two battalions of British Light Infantry, two battalions of

British Grenadiers, the wing companies of the British Guards, and the 37th, 42nd, and 43rd Regiments, the other Hessian Grenadier Battalions, and the Landgraf and Leib Regiments. The fleet assembled at Whitestone. It appears the preparations are for going to Rhode Island, where the French fleet noted above in June of this year, had not only captured the harbor, but had also landed the troops which it had on board.

The 26th and 27th of July - The rest of the fleet came up the East River. Travel through Hellgate with large ships is very dangerous, and therefore proceeded very slowly until all the ships had passed through. As soon as all the ships had arrived here, the fleet set sail at six o'clock in the evening, and traveled up the East River. The fleet consisted of three frigates, a war sloop, and 62 transports and store ships.

The 28th of July - This morning we lay at anchor in Huntington Bay, on Long Island, and the ships received orders to take on water. Two frigates from our fleet continued up the East River, supposedly following Admiral Arbuthnot, who had gone with the warships into the ocean, near the east end of Long Island, or the exit from the Sound or East River.

The 29th of July - The fleet remained in Huntington Bay, and was busy taking on water.

The 30th of July - The frigates which sailed ahead day before yesterday, returned. A signal to sail was made immediately, and we returned to Whitestone. We dropped anchor there about eleven o'clock in the morning. The troops received orders, that as soon as the field equipment could be brought from New York, they were to land on Long Island, but the ships were to maneuver. We heard that the two frigates, mentioned above, had been driven back.

The 1st and 2nd of August - The troops were landed on Long Island, and entered camp in the area of Whitestone and New Flushing. The Hessian Grenadier Brigade remained near the landing place.

The 9th of November - From the start of this month on, the troops in camp began to enter winter quarters, the Linsing and Lengercke Grenadier Battalions at Jamaica, and the Loewenstein and Graf Grenadier Battalions at New Flushing. The officers entered houses, the non-commissioned officers and privates, however, entered huts built at both places, after we had been in camp at Whitestone from early August until today. On 8 October, a corps of troops at this place, under the command of General Leslie, embarked. Of the Hessians, only a detachment of Jaegers and the Bose Regiment were included. In addition to these, there were two battalions of English Guards, the 82nd Regiment, and Colonel Fanning's Corps, and the rest of the 17th Regiment, plus the light infantry companies of the provincial corps under the command of Colonel Watson. This corps landed at Portsmouth in Virginia, and later left that post, and went to Charleston.

The 30th of November - The Graf and Lengercke Grenadier Battalions received orders to be prepared to embark.

The 11th of December - The Graf Grenadier Battalion marched out of New Flushing on Long Island, crossed the East River at Hellgate, and relieved the 80th Regiment at Fort Knyphausen on York Island. The 38th Regiment relieved Robinson's Corps at Moore's Hill. In addition to these, the Donop and 78th Regiments were at the fort.

The 11th, 12th, and 13th of December - One hundred Hessian jaegers, commanded by Captain Ewald, the 80th Regiment, Robinson's Corps, and the Queen's Rangers, all under the command of General [Benedict] Arnold, embarked on an expedition to Virginia. General Arnold came over to our army from the rebels in the past September. He was under suspicion of having joined the royal party, as he had made a great many enemies among the rebels during the past year. It is said that during this time, he had been in secret correspondence with General Clinton, and had sought a favorable opportunity to surrender a large number of the troops under his command. No more favorable opportunity had presented itself than the one of his being commandant of Fort Defiance [West Point] on the North River. The plan to surrender this fort and the troops therein was developed in the following manner: Our side was to attack, and the commandant would immediately surrender. The adjutant general, Major [John] Andre, secretly left the guard ship *Vulture,* lying in the North River, during the night, and fortunately reached General Arnold in Fort Defiance. According to the agreement, and the plan outlined to him, Major Andre, dressed as a local native, returned by land. He accidentally encountered some militiamen, who questioned him, and finally held him as a spy, even though he had a pass from General Arnold. Andre was taken before General Washington, who was in the area, and Arnold, who learned of Major Andre's arrest, quickly went in a boat to the above mentioned guard ship lying in the North River, and eventually arrived safely in New York. He was made a brigadier general with the British troops, and received the above command. Major Andre was court-martialed as a spy, and despite all of General Clinton's efforts, hanged. We received news from the troops embarked with General Arnold, that they had landed in Virginia.

Several good reports were received from Lord Cornwallis concerning successes achieved over the enemy in the southern provinces.

1781

January - At the start of this year, a mutiny broke out in the rebel army. Between 2,000 and 3,000 men, under the command of General [Henry] Knox, left their winter quarters at Morristown in New Jersey. These malcontents moved from Morristown toward Elizabethtown, took a secure position on a height, and demanded their many months back pay, in hard cash, better uniform items, and better provisions. Therefore, three Hessian and two British grenadier battalions, the Jaegers, and two British light infantry battalions were transferred from Long Island to Staten Island today, in order to be nearer these malcontents. General Clinton himself went to Staten Island, and commenced a correspondence with them. Reportedly our side promised them all their back pay, if they came over to us. However, they refused this offer, as it was never their intention to cross over to us, but they would remain neutral; and return to their homes. These malcontents have been reconciled with Congress and General Washington, and rejoined the rebel army again as the result of promises, exhortations, and being given part of their pay.

The 10th of January - The above mentioned corps of our army returned to winter quarters on Long Island, having accomplished nothing.

The 18th of February 1781 - In a letter dated Wissenstein, 16 November 1780, from His Serene Highness, to Lieutenant Colonel Graf, which was received today, Captains Hessenmueller, Neumann, and Bodewere, promoted to major. The first received the grenadier company of the Buenau Regiment. Major Neumann also received a company, and was assigned as major of the Seitz Regiment. Major Bode was transferred to the Angelelli Regiment, and Staff Captain [Gregorius] Salzmann of the latter regiment, received his company [in the Graf Grenadier Battalion.]

The 4th of March - The 76th Regiment of Highlanders, which had previously been in huts on Laurel Hill, marched to New York in order to embark for Virginia. That regiment joined a small corps of troops under the command of General [William] Phillips, going to the previously noted province. The 76th Regiment relieved the 57th Regiment, and the Combined Battalion, commanded by Major [Johann Friedrich Georg] von Stein.

The 30th of April - The Combined Battalion marched out of the huts here, and marched off to Denyse's Ferry, on Long Island.

The 14th of June - Until this time, the Graf

Grenadier Battalion remained quietly in winter quarters. The Young Lossberg Regiment relieved our battalion today, and it marched to New York to join the other three grenadier battalions in camp near the city.

July - The start of this month, the French troops under the command of General [Donatian Vimeur, Comte de] Rochambeau joined the army of General Washington on the North River, and gradually approached our outposts near Kingsbridge. Near Fort Knyphausen, our Jaegers had a scrimmage with them. Captain von Rau of the British [sic] Jaegers had died during a patrol some days previously. The enemy bivouacked near our outposts, so close to Harlem Creek that the jaegers this side of Harlem Creek had to vacate their camp below Fort Knyphausen at night. The army Refugees, who had built huts on the other side of Harlem Creek at Morrisania, were plundered by the enemy, and many taken captive, wounded, or killed. Everyone on the other side of Harlem Creek had to retreat to this side. We no longer occupied anything, but Redoubt Number 8, which the enemy was very near. We remained still, rested, and did not exert ourselves, except for firing several cannon shots at the enemy. After a stay of several days, the enemy again marched away from Kingsbridge without having undertaken anything. They went farther up the North River. As soon as the enemy had departed, pontoons were brought from New York to Kingsbridge to demonstrate that our side was not completely idle and onlookers to the situation.

The 12th of August - The recruits who arrived from Hesse with Colonel [Ferdinand Ludwig] von Benning, were landed and assigned [among the regiments]. The Graf Grenadier Battalion received 33 men. Uniform items and field equipment also arrived with the transports.

The 18th of August - The Grenadier Brigade moved out from New York, and marched into camp at McGowan's Pass. The Buenau Regiment was also brought up the North River from Staten Island in small vessels, and camped ahead of us on John's Hill.

The 25th of August - The Hessian Grenadier Brigade marched from McGowan's Pass to New York, and was carried across the East River from near the shipyard to Long Island. The Linsing and Lengercke Battalions went into camp at Yellow Hook, and Loewenstein and Graf Battalions at Denyse's Ferry.

The 28th of August - We received orders to be prepared to embark, for which purpose the ships lay in The Narrows, and on which the following distribution was intended:

The Linsing Grenadier Battalion on *Lord Howe*, 294 tons, and *Providence*, 264 tons, flying a blue vane over one white ball at the main.

The Lengercke Grenadier Battalion on *Peggy*, 360 tons, and *Grace*, 278 tons, flying a blue and white vane at the main.

The Loewenstein Grenadier Battalion on *Alicia*, 320 tons, and *Hope*, 286 tons, flying a blue and white vane at the fore.

The Graf Grenadier Battalion on *Alexander*, 430 tons, and *Wisk*, 272 tons, flying a blue vane at the fore.

Major General von Kospoth on the *Caldonia,* 209 tons, flying a pendant at the main.

The order was signed by [Frederick] Mackenzie, Deputy Adjutant General.

<u>The 29th of August</u> - Today the embarkation order was countermanded.

<u>The 5th of September</u> - The Hessian Grenadiers were embarked on the ships listed under 28 August. The wagon horses and artillery horses had been delivered previously to the Quartermaster General

Department. The wagons and equipment and the artillery were taken aboard ship. Only a very little baggage was taken on board. The women had to remain in the huts at Denyse's Ferry, where a non-commissioned officer from each battalion commanded. Because here at Denyse's Ferry our camp was located on an old swamp, we suffered a great many sick. Even Lieutenant Colonel Graf had to remain behind sick, with a fever at Denyse's Ferry. During this time, in which a corps of troops was involved in embarking, General Arnold, who had returned from Virginia on his own, went with a small corps of troops to New England, and destroyed New London and its harbor, and several forts. During the conquest of Fort Griswold, the 40th and 54th Regiments suffered severe losses. No one from Hesse accompanied this expedition, except 100 jaegers, under the command of Captain von Wangenheim.

In addition to the Hessian Grenadier Brigade, two battalions of English grenadiers, the 22nd, 37th, and 47th Regiments, a detachment of 400 jaegers, under the command of Colonel [Ludwig Johann Adolf] von Wurmb, the Prince Charles and the Leib Regiments, and a number of the recruits for units in Virginia, were embarked today at Denyse's Ferry and New York.

<u>The 16th of September</u> - It is said that Lord

Cornwallis has been closely confined by the enemy at Yorktown in Virginia, and that these embarked troops are meant to be a relief force. General Washington and Rochambeau have marched there with the troops under their command, and the French fleet is supposedly much stronger than ours. At present our fleet lies here in the harbor, and repairs the damage inflicted by the French fleet at the start of this month, in an engagement on the Virginia coast. In the engagement, we lost the ship *Terrible*. Because it had not only developed leaks on the voyage coming from the West Indies, but had suffered greatly in the above engagement, it was set on fire during the night and burned, so as not to fall into enemy hands.

The 21st of September - All the above troops disembarked at Cole's Ferry on Staten Island, and entered camp around the Watering Place, after having lain at anchor on the ships, between Long Island and Staten Island, from the fifth until today.

The 23rd of September - Lieutenant Colonel Graf, who had been left behind sick, died of putrid fever at Denyse's Ferry.

The 13th of September - Lieutenant Colonel Graf was buried quietly at New Utrecht on Long Island, because there are no longer any troops there at present, except the Hanau Free Corps, which is at Brooklyn Ferry, and too far away to render funeral honors.

The 25th of September - Major [Friedrich] Platte reported to the vacant Graf Battalion, and on the orders of Lieutenant General von Knyphausen, took over command of the unit for the time being.

The 29th of September - We received news that all of the troops camped here are to be embarked on board warships.

The 2nd of October - The Hessian Grenadier Brigade moved out from the Watering Place and marched to Richmond, the Jaegers to Blazing Star, and the two British grenadier battalions to Phillip's Point. [Possibly this should be Billop's Point.] The rest of the troops, which were to be embarked, remained in their former camps.

The 9th of October - We marched back from the above places into our former camps at the Watering Place.

The 11th of October - All the troops embarked in the previously designated transport ships, which lay at Cole's Ferry on Staten Island.

The 16th and 17th of October - Until today the transport ships lay at anchor at the mentioned place. The warships, which had been repaired and supplied with provisions and water, came here, this time, from New York, and then went to Sandy Hook. During the two days, all the transport ships, on which the troops were embarked, joined the warships at Sandy Hook.

The 18th and 19th of October - The troops on board the transport ships were embarked on the warships. The Hessian Grenadier Brigade went aboard the following ships:

1) Linsing Grenadier Battalion on *Alcide*, 276 men and one cannon.

2) Lengercke Grenadier Battalion on *Resolution*, 276 men and one cannon.

3) Loewenstein Grenadier Battalion on *Centurion*, 276 men and one cannon.

4) Vacant Graf Grenadier Battalion on *Shrewsbury*, 276 men and one cannon.

5) From Linsing and Loewenstein on *Centurion*, 276 men and one cannon.

6) From Lengercke and Vacant Graf on *Montague*, 276 men and one cannon.

7) From Linsing and Loewenstein, on *Perseverence,* 50 men and one cannon.

8) From Vacant Graf on *Sybilla,* 30 men and one cannon.

Major General von Kospoth was on the *Invincible.*

Because the Grenadier Brigade had very many sick officers, nineteen Brunswick and Hanau officers were assigned to do duty on this expedition. No baggage was allowed to be taken except what a servant could carry in an emergency. The women, of whom not one was allowed to accompany the expedition, remained with the baggage on the transport ships, which returned to New York. The entire fleet consisted of those ships in the accompanying list. (See the following charts.) [The list follows this page.] The land troops are not included in the indicated number of crew members in the list. Therefore, the ships were very full of people, and the accommodations were greatly reduced. The officers were put up in the ward room with the naval officers, and during the night had to sleep on the floor. Non-commissioned officers and privates were put by the heavy cannons, and had to find places to sleep between the cannons. The staff officers and senior captains, for the most part, were quartered with the [ships'] captains. On the evening of the nineteenth the

Lit. A. [243]

Line of Battle.

The Princessa to lead with the Starboard & the Bedford with the Larboard Tacks on Board.

Frigates	Rate	Ships	Commanders	Guns	Men	Division
			Rear Admiral Drake			
Sybell	3	Princessa	Captn. Knatchball	70	577	
Richmond	"	Alcide	" Thomson	74	600	Robert
"	,	Lion	" Fooch	64	500	Digby
"	,	Canada	" Cornwallis	74	600	Esquire Rear Admiral of the
			Rear Admiral Digby			
Perseverance to repeat Signals	2	Prince George	Captn. Williams	96	768	Red &c.
Lucifer Fire Ship.	3	Resolution	" Lord Manners	74	600	
	,	Intrepid	" Molloy	64	500	
Felicity	,	Montagu	" Bowen	74	600	Thomas
Pearl	4	Warwick	" Elphinstone	50	350	Graves Esquire
"	3	Prince William	" Wilkinson	64	500	Rear admiral of the
Rattle Snake	4	Centaur	" Inglefield	74	650	
Carysford	,	Europa	" Child	64	500	
Valcono Fire ship	,	Robust	" Cosby			
			Latus	842	6745	

Continuat.

Frigates	Rates	Ships.	Commanders	Guns	Men	Division
		Transport		842	6745	
			Rear Admiral Graves.			
Orphens to repeat Signals	2	London	Capt. Hampthorn & Morice	98	800	Red, Commander in Cheff &c. &c.
Amphion	3	Royal Oak	" Burnet	74	600	
Conflagration Fire Schip.	"	America	" Thomson	64	500	
Menior	"	Shrewsbury	" Knight	74	600	
"	"	Torbay	" Gidion	74	600	
			Rear Admiral Graves			
Blonde	4	Adamant	Capt. Graves	50	350	
Lively	3	Ajax	" Charrington	74	550	
"	"	Prudent	" Barckley	64	500	
Salamander Fire Ship	"	Monarche	" Reynolds.	74	600	Sir Samuel Hood
			Rear Admiral Hood.			
Pegasus to repeat Signals	2	Barfleur	Capt. Hood	96	768	Baronet Rear Admiral of the Blue &c. &c.
Ostrich	3	Invincible	" Saxton	74	600	
	"	Belliqueux	" Brine	64	500	
"	"	Alfred	" Bayne	74	600	
Nymphe	"		Commandeur Affleck			
St. Margaretha	"	Bedford	Capt. Graves.	74	617	
				1944	1530	

To Capt. Knight of His Majestys Ship the Shrewsbury.

Given on Board His Majestys Ship London in the North River of Newyork den 13. Oct. 1781.
Thomas Graves.

fleet sailed out to sea as an even larger fleet from England entered near Sandy Hook.

The 20th of October - This evening the sea was so rough and the wind so strong that finally a storm arose. It was possible now to differentiate between a transport and a warship in stormy weather. We found the stormy weather not half so strong as it would have been for us on a transport ship, had we been on one. The only worry which we now had on our ship was for the main mast. Because *Shrewsbury* had been severely damaged in the action with the French on the Chesapeake Bay, and had suffered the loss of the middle mast, it had received a new one at New York. However, this one was too heavy, and everyone feared it would break.

The 21st of October - Toward noon the storm abated and we sailed on a calm sea.

The 25th of October - We saw land to the south. Toward noon, the ship was about twelve leagues from land. According to the noon sighting, we were at 37°32' north latitude, and not far from the mouth of the Chesapeake Bay. Although we had the most favorable wind for entering the bay, we lay to before the wind. Everything aboard the ship was made ready for an action, and we expected that such would occur today, although no enemy ships were to be seen.

Therefore, the ship's officers thought we would enter the bay today, or this evening. Our ship's captain went aboard the admiral's ship *London* this afternoon, and returned to us with the most astonishing, unpleasant news, that Lord Cornwallis and his army had surrendered already, on the nineteenth of this month, and been made prisoners of war.

The 26th of October - The fleet continued to cruise outside the bay, but we saw no enemy ships.

The 27th of October - We still continued to cruise outside the bay and saw several French ships sailing in Hampton Roads. They would not risk coming out, however. The *Warwick* was sent in, but the French showed no desire to let it approach, and therefore withdrew farther into the bay. From the top of the mast, 29 French ships-of-the-line could be counted, at anchor in Hampton Roads. According to reports received, the entire French fleet consisted of 36 ships-of-the-line.

The 28th and 29th of October - We cruised continuously outside the bay, and saw enemy frigates doing the same inside the bay. As soon as ours approached them, the French frigates withdrew. Despite the French fleet being much larger than ours, the French showed no sign of desiring to engage in battle with ours, but remained peacefully inside the bay. About two o'clock in the afternoon, the admiral signaled for the ships to assemble, and for all the frigates to join the fleet. After the signal was answered, all the ships set sail and steered toward the north. Apparently we will return to New York.

The 2nd of November - At nightfall we dropped anchor at Sandy Hook. Occasionally on our return we had had stormy weather. The last night was especially unpleasant. The fleet was completely scattered and only reassembled about noon today. This fruitless and too late undertaken expedition was now ended, and we are again to go aboard the transport ships lying here for that purpose. If we had gone on the warships fourteen days earlier, Lord Cornwallis probably would not have been captured, and all our hopes for success in the southern area would not have been destroyed. The second Burgoyning will undoubtedly contribute to an unfortunate conclusion to the war. Before we leave the warship, I can not fail to mention that we owe the navy the greatest appreciation for the courtesy extended to us. As long as we were on board the ship, we were treated not only splendidly with food and drink, but they sought to make it as pleasant for us as circumstances would allow. We brought no bedding with us, and instead received sailcloth and flags as blankets. All the navy and marine officers lent us their overcoats. Beside the ship's captain, Captain Knight, on the ship there were five naval officers and a volunteer from the warship *Terrible*, sunk in the last action, serving as lieutenants, and a captain and two lieutenants from the marines. We paid nothing for the accommodations provided by our comrades. The strictest organization, discipline, activity, and the exceptional cleanliness aboard the warships merits not only notice, but also wonderment. If these rules were rigorously enforced among the troops on the transport ships, we would not have had so much sickness. It is astonishing to see how many men, how many cannons, how much armament, munitions, provisions, how much ship building materials, and other items are to be found on a 74-gun ship, and yet, everywhere there is comfort and space. All this is the result of good and strict discipline. Nothing more could be wished for, than that this good organization and system could be exactly observed in building houses. There would be no reason to complain about houses built in this manner failing to please the eye, symmetrically from without, and giving comfort within.

The 3rd of November - We were transferred from the warships to the transports in rather stormy weather.

The 8th of November - We spent the time until today on the transport ships due to contrary wind, in a terrible situation, because we had no provisions, and to make matters worse, the weather was very cold.

The 9th of November - Part of the vacant Graf Grenadier Battalion was landed. Several of the ships were driven out into the sea, and returned to Denyse's Ferry on Long Island, where all the troops were landed, and we entered our former camp.

The 14th of November - The Grenadier Brigade moved into winter quarters in New York. In addition to the brigade, the Landgraf and Knyphausen Regiments (the rest of whom had returned from Canada during our absence), the Buenau Regiment, and also the 40th Regiment, were in New York, as well as the Combined Battalion, under the command of Colonel [Johann Friedrich] von Cochenhausen.

Thus ended the unfortunate campaign of 1781. If it will be the last, as many believe, only the future can tell.

1782

This year's winter quarters were occupied by the grenadiers and all the troops, undisturbed, in the places which had been assigned to them, without any changes. Nothing much was heard of war, except that since the arrival of Admiral [Robert] Digby, who was assigned his station in New York, and subsequently the entire east coast of the rebel provinces, many more, and more valuable prizes were taken from the enemy than had been taken by the previous admirals. The warships were no longer allowed to lie idle in the harbor for months at a time, and a day never passed without the results of this aggressive policy being observed. The prizes were brought in daily, and it had progressed so far, that ships often had to lie for a long time in the enemy harbors, before they could risk sailing out. In the public press, complaints were read daily, that the loaded ships dared not leave, and the rebels therefore suffered great inconvenience. If all the admirals had been so aggressive from the beginning, they would have not only enjoyed the same advantages as Admiral Digby, but the rebels' commerce would have been greatly restricted, and possibly their credit would have diminished.

<u>March</u> - At the beginning of this month, Lieutenant General Sir Guy Carleton came from

England and assumed command over the army.

The 7th of May - Lieutenant General Sir Henry Clinton and Lieutenant General von Knyphausen returned to Europe. Lieutenant General [Friedrich Wilhelm] von Lossberg assumed command over the Hessian troops in North America. During the departure of the two generals, the troops had to fall out and form lines, between which they marched from the headquarters, to the ship on which they embarked, and the cannons at Fort George were fired.

June - During the middle of this month, the troops entered camp. The Hessian Grenadier Brigade entered camp at Greenwich, two miles from New York.

The 13th of August - The garrison from Savannah arrived in this region. With the evacuation of that place, we also lost the occupation of Georgia, which had been held since the start of 1779 at such a great cost, and the loss of so many men. The troops, which contained no Hessian units, except the Knoblauch Regiment, were quartered in New York and on Long Island.

September - During this month Lieutenant Colonel Platte received the previously vacant Graf Grenadier Battalion from His Serene Highness, and hereafter it will have the name Platte.

The 23rd of September - Lieutenant [Christian Ernst] Kleinsteuber died. At the end of this month, all the troops moved to York Island and camped in three lines, one behind the other, between the Five and Nine Mile Stones.

October - During the middle of this month, all the troops marched from their camps to the plain and heights near Harlem, in three columns, and were inspected by His Royal Highness, Prince William Henry, the generals, and the admirals. Because it is the hurricane season, the West Indies fleet lay in the harbor at New York during this time, under the command of Admirals [Hugh] Pigot and [Sir Samuel] Hood.

The 4th of November - The troops marched into their designated winter quarters. The Grenadier Brigade was in and near New York, the Platte Grenadier Battalion in Greenwich and Bloomingdale, the Lengercke Grenadier Battalion on the East River, and the other two in New York.

Captain Fritsch of this battalion died at the end of this month.

We ended this undisturbed, and in the middle of war, peaceful year, in which we undertook as little as our enemy. Nothing was missing except an open passage between the lines of each side through which everyone would be allowed to pass back and forth. Otherwise, no one would have known whether there was peace or war.

1783

January - In this month, at the beginning, the garrison from Charleston also arrived in New York. We thus lost all hold on the southern provinces of North America, except for St. Augustine, in Florida.

March - At the end of this month we received the news that the thirteen rebel provinces had been declared free from England. This news spread a general consternation within the army and among the residents residing within our lines. For the Loyalists this was the most unpleasant news, as they had never expected England to do this.

August - Since the past spring, nothing more has occurred, except that there has been constant activity moving the Royalists from here to Nova Scotia, Canada, the West Indies, and Great Britain. The persons going to Nova Scotia and Canada received provisions for one year, and a tract of unoccupied land. Although in fact, these people, according to the preliminary peace articles, were to have their land and possessions, which they had abandoned, restored, the rebels would not agree to this, and they were persecuted in the most cruel manner when they sought to see their belongings, or even to inquire about them. The oppression to which these unfortunate people, even those who did not participate in the war, were subjected to, passes all description. Nothing was left for them except to seek peace and security in the rough, wild, and undeveloped regions of Nova Scotia, Canada, or other places to which one transport after another was sent. Several Hessian officers and soldiers also took their discharge and went there in order to settle. A captain who went there received 3,000 acres of land, a subaltern, 1,500 acres, a non-commissioned officer or private, 150 acres, and each was given a proportionate amount of land. All officers and men of the newly raised English corps were placed on half pay for life, and received the above portions of land in Nova Scotia and Canada.

In the city of Port Roseway or Shelburne Town, named for Lord Shelburne, under whose ministry the Peace of Paris [1783] was made, reportedly now consists of nearly 500 houses, although in the past spring there were none. It lies on Fundy Bay, and supposedly everything should grow there, which grows from 52° to the more northerly part of Germany. Because of the money which the immigrants take there, because of the healthy climate, and because of the favorable location for access to shipping, it can be seen that there is every appearance it will become one of the most prosperous provinces in America. Lieutenant [Joseph Henrich] Wiederhold, Ensign [Gottlieb] Grebe, and seventeen grenadiers of the

Platte Grenadier Battalion took their discharges in order to settle in Nova Scotia.

The 11th of August - The first division of Hessians, under the command of Major General von Kospoth, consisting of the Ditfurth, Knyphausen, Bose, Vacant Hereditary Prince, Angelelli, Knoblauch, Buenau, and Benning Regiments, embarked to return to Europe.

September - During the month we were busy loading all war materials, ammunition, provisions, cannons, and similar items. A large amount of cavalry and infantry uniform items were sold by the British at auction. Wagons and horses and their equipment were in part publicly sold, and in part, sent to Nova Scotia. During the month, 2nd Lieutenant [Reinhard] Junck of Captain Sandrock's Company, died.

The 26th of October - We received orders to march to McGowan's Pass tomorrow.

The 27th of October - We marched here, after spending almost one year, peacefully, in our quarters on the Hudson River. The Jaegers, who were lying here, cleared out a barracks for us.

The 4th of November - We received orders to be prepared to go aboard ship, which was firmly set to take place on the eighth of this month, in order to return to Europe.

The 8th of November - The Linsing, Loewenstein, and Platte Grenadier Battalions, and the Leib, Hereditary Prince, and Prince Charles Regiments went aboard ship. All the troops were under the command of Major General [Friedrich Wilhelm] von Wurmb, who embarked on the ninth. The Platte Grenadier Battalion went on board the transport ships *Palliser* and *Ranger.* After having spent seven years and a half month in America, we departed. We embarked at the same place on the North River, near New York, where we had first dropped anchor in America, in 1776. The only Hessian troops remaining in America are the Jaeger Corps, the Lengercke Grenadier Battalion, and the Young Lossberg and Donop Regiments, which have already been ordered to be prepared to embark aboard ship.

After our departure, New York was no longer as heavily populated as it had been five or six years previously. The population had been reduced by nearly one-half, since the past spring. The reduction in trade was also connected with this. The richest and most important merchants had fled to England and other lands for fear of the new government. With these and the many departed Loyalists, most of the available money also departed. Our fleet also took away a considerable sum of guineas, which was also disadvantageous to the commercial situation. Instead of all the houses in New York being full of residents, and there being difficulty in renting a place to live, now on the other hand, many houses and stores stand empty.

In spite of this, the commerce of New York is still of considerable importance as a result of the evacuation, and is even greater than it will be for some years to come. The people from the countryside appear to have a great scarcity of all items, and daily come to New York in great numbers to make purchases. There is a shortage of money for buying these items, so they must bring their products, consisting mainly of foodstuffs, to the market. Naturally, due to the great amount of foodstuffs brought to the market on land and by water, the prices have fallen as much as 500 percent.

Manufactured products, however, have retained their former prices, as America must obtain these items, without exception, from Europe and other parts of the world. America is short of the number of inhabitants necessary, in looking back, to fully populate and develop such a large area in this part of the world. Therefore, there is no possibility that manufacturing in this part of the world will prosper, unless new inhabitants come from other lands. Due to the rebellion, the population has greatly decreased. By adopting bad policies, which have driven the Loyalists from house and home to Nova Scotia and other regions, and the severe prosecution, the population has not only diminished, but many vacated estates must naturally cause the devaluation of the farms, and force the price to be greatly reduced.

Despite America being naturally fertile due to the favorable and mild climate, the land does not produce nearly as well as the land in Europe. It can not be denied that cultivation of the land is not carried on as industrially at present, as is done in England or Germany. But, as the very best cultivated acres do not produce nearly as well as in England or Germany, the conclusion can be drawn that in the future, when these lands are settled, it will still not be able to fulfill all its needs, but will be obliged to have the necessities supplied by foreign lands. It must also be considered that the West Indies presently get their requirements from the united northern provinces.

The great debt which America, or more correctly, The Thirteen United Provinces, has hanging around its neck as a result of the war, and the maintenance of a country, will naturally necessitate the taxes and duties being very high, a situation, which at the present time, is not accepted without complaint. At the same time, the good fortune and prosperous living conditions of the citizens will be less advantageous, and not as easy, nor with such good financial results, as before the rebellion began.

The 12th of November - We weighed anchor in the North River and sailed to Sandy Hook.

The 13th of November - Toward eleven o'clock, the commodore's ship *Dolphin*, 44 guns, approached from New York, and at once gave the signal for the fleet to get underway. The anchor was raised and the fleet sailed out to sea. Including the commodore and several store ships, the fleet consisted of 25 sail. Our course was toward the southeast.

The 21st of November - Since the last date, we have continued to sail to the southeast, and by today's observation, we were at 35°58' north latitude. The weather was pleasant and warm, even though we had daily rain and occasionally snow showers. We had continuously strong wind blasts since leaving Sandy Hook, with very high seas, so that the waves washed over the deck. This caused us not only many unpleasant days, but we also lost much of the foodstuff which we had purchased. Today our fleet consisted of only seventeen sail, the others having been scattered in stormy weather on the nineteenth of this month.

The 22nd of November - We were at 36°40' north latitude according to the noon observation and have sailed 42 miles since yesterday, in a more northerly direction.

The 25th of November - Of the above seventeen ships, seven became separated in a storm last night, including the commodore's ship *Dolphin*. The other ten ships, among which is still the agent's ship, assembled again today, and lay to before the wind in the hope that the missing ships would rejoin us. As no more ships were to be seen, the rest set sail toward evening.

The 26th of November - This morning not a single other ship was to be seen. The ship's captain therefore put on as much sail as the hard, stormy weather would permit, and continued to steer his own course. Toward noon we saw the agent's ship ahead of us, and four other ships at a great distance toward the south. This afternoon we had weak wind, and nearly a calm. Toward evening we lost sight of the above ships.

The 29th of November - We could no longer see a

single ship from our fleet, and steered our course toward the northeast, for which we had favorable but also very strong west and northwest wind. The sea was very high so that waves constantly ran over the deck, which resulted from continuous squalls and rain showers. According to the noon observation, we were at 39°17' north latitude. This evening, according to the ship's captain, we had completed one-half of our voyage to Lizard Point, in England.

The 30th of November - We sailed 170 English miles from noon yesterday until twelve o'clock today. Weather and wind were as yesterday, but somewhat stronger. The sea was very rough. We could only raise one sail on the foremast and one sail on the mainmast, and with them we sailed seven, eight, and even nine miles per hour. As a natural consequence, the motion of the ship was very great, and therefore all the more unpleasant for us. By today's observation, we were at 43°05' north latitude.

The 1st of December - From noon yesterday until noon today, we sailed 168 miles with a continuously strong storm. According to the observation, we were at 44°17' north latitude, and steered more to the east than to the north.

The 2nd of December - According to the noon

observation, we were at 44°44' north latitude, and had sailed 143 miles since yesterday. Today the sea was somewhat smoother and the wind not as strong as yesterday, but we again had several squalls. During the afternoon, we saw a large ship to the southward, which steered the same course to the east as we did. It appeared to be a warship, and our captain thought it to be our commodore's ship *Dolphin.* However, because of high seas and foggy weather, it was lost from sight toward evening.

The 3rd of December - Last night was the most uncomfortable and stormiest that we had yet had. We could not take a noon observation because of the stormy and foggy weather. According to the logbook, we sailed 184 miles from noon yesterday until noon today. We still had the same wind as yesterday. We saw nothing more today of the ship mentioned yesterday. The sea was so high, it was nearly impossible to see half an English mile. Our ship's captain assured us that the sea had been higher at eleven o'clock last night than he had ever seen it in his lifetime. Three times he figured the water would come over the stern, and onto the quarterdeck. Three times he had entered the cabin thinking the water had found its way through the window. He was glad that he had found all of us asleep.

<u>The 4th of December</u> - We were at 47°13' north latitude. From noon yesterday until noon today, we sailed 134 miles. The weather was pleasant, the sea smoother, but we could notice by the increasing cold that we had gone farther north.

<u>The 5th of December</u> - According to the noon observation, we were at 48°02' north latitude today. Since noon yesterday we had sailed 113 miles.

<u>The 6th of December</u> - Last night we had the most severe storm we have had yet, accompanied by contrary wind. It was foggy and rained hard. We tacked but made no forward progress.

<u>The 7th of December</u> - This morning the wind was better, and by noon today we had sailed 64 miles.

<u>The 8th of December</u> - According to the noon observation, we were at 49°41' north latitude. We steered directly toward the English Channel. Since yesterday afternoon, with a weak, but favorable wind, and with many sails, we covered 120 miles. This afternoon we carried as many sails as we possibly could.

<u>The 9th of December</u> - We had no sun at noon today due to an overcast. From yesterday noon until

this noon, we sailed 103 miles, according to the logbook. Early today, at daybreak, we saw a two-masted ship to the northwest. It steered the same course that we did. Supposedly, it was onc of the store ships of our fleet. We lost sight of it toward noon, because our ship sailed much better.

The 10th of December - Because of thick weather, we could not take a sighting again today. We steered east-southeast. Since yesterday noon we had sailed 156 miles. Toward evening we took a sounding, but found no bottom at 175 fathoms.

The 11th of December - We had contrary and calm winds. Because of the dull weather, we still could not see the sun, and did not know where we were. The ship's captain and everyone on the ship were in bad humor. At daybreak, we saw a three-masted ship ahead of us, which we overtook at about twelve o'clock. The captain of that ship did not know where he was either, because he had not been able to take a sighting since the eighth. The captain of that ship came aboard our ship, and told us he had come from Virginia five weeks ago, with a cargo of turpentine and tobacco for Cork, Ireland. In the storm, noted on the sixth of this month, the captain found it necessary to throw the entire cargo, consisting of 400 barrels of tobacco and turpentine, overboard, because the ship had been very close to sinking, and he was able to save his ship only with the greatest effort.

The 12th of December - The wind was contrary and the weather as yesterday. We had to steer a completely contrary course toward the southwest. To our great disappointment, again today, we had no sun. We could no longer see the ship seen yesterday.

The 13th of December - At daybreak this morning, we saw a large ship at a great distance from us. Our ship's captain recognized it as the transport ship *Duke of Richmond*, on which was the Linsing Grenadier Battalion. We immediately made a signal that our ship belonged to the fleet. Upon receiving an acknowledgement to our signal, we sailed toward that ship, and overtook it at twelve o'clock. Already on the nineteenth of November, with the missing ships mentioned on the 21st, it had become separated from the fleet, and had seen no other ship of our fleet since that time. Colonel [Otto Friedrich Wilhelm] von Linsingen requested that an officer from out ship be sent over. Upon his rcturn, we heard that the *Duke of Richmond* had taken 160 men off an East India Company ship, which sank on the fifth of this month, and saved them. Our ship's captain told us that he had heard of this misfortune. The loss, including private belongings, amounted to 300,000 pounds. We had pleasant weather today, but weak and contrary wind. According to today's observation, we were at 49°48' north latitude.

The 14th of December - We were at 49°23' north latitude. Wind and weather were as yesterday. Several officers and some of those from the unfortunate East India Company ship came from the *Duke of Richmond* for a visit on our ship.

The 15th of December - This morning we saw two very small single-masted vessels at a distance, one of which came to us. It was from Malaga, bound for Marly, loaded with wine, lemons, figs, and oranges, but had absolutely no more provisions on board, and therefore received some from the *Duke of Richmond.* It had been out for 55 days, and had had contrary wind for the last fifteen days. According to the noon observation, we were at 48°35' north latitude. The wind was somewhat better than yesterday.

The 16th of December - This morning we spoke to a Dutch brigantine, which had sailed six months ago from Demrara, in the West Indies. It had absolutely no provisions, and was supplied with some by the *Duke of Richmond.* It sailed in company with us thereafter. Toward noon, we spoke with a transport ship *Nancy.* It sailed from Halifax four weeks ago, with English troops bound for Portsmouth. Despite cruising in this northern latitude for ten days, it had not spoken to any ship from our fleet. The weather today was dark, unpleasant, and cold. The wind, however, was better than yesterday. We were unable to take a noon observation, but must be at about 49°09' north latitude.

The 17th of December - We were at 49°01' north latitude. We again saw a strange ship in the distance. Because of a wind calm, however, it could not draw near to us, even though it steered toward us and we laid still. The three last named ships continued in our company.

The 18th of December - We were at 49°58' north latitude. The previously mentioned Dutch ship from Demrara, was lost from our fleet last night, but on the other hand, we discovered another strange ship behind us. The wind was rather strong today, but contrary.

The 19th of December - We were at 49°31' north latitude. The wind was contrary. We saw several ships in the distance, to our left and right.

The 20th of December - We could not take a noon sighting, and had to tack with a contrary wind.

The 21st of December Last night the wind swung in our favor, to the southwest, but was very weak. Because of overcast weather, to our regret, we could not take a noon observation. At four o'clock in the afternoon, we found bottom for the first time, at 85 fathoms.

The 22nd of December - According to the noon observation, we were at 49°15' north latitude. This morning we found bottom at seventy fathoms. Since noon yesterday we have sailed 158 miles. Toward noon, we saw four ships to the north, and our ship's captain said that one was our commodore's ship, and the others apparently belonged to our fleet, also.

The 23rd of December - Toward noon today we saw Lizard Point, in England, which was the first land since America. The *Duke of Richmond* separated from us this morning, and steered closer to the French coast. Therefore, we continued on our course alone. We saw a great many ships entering and leaving the Channel, but none from our fleet.

The 24th of December - At daybreak this morning, we passed quite near Point Portland, which lay some miles to the north of us. Toward ten o'clock in the morning, we saw the Isle of Wight lying before us. By nightfall, we had left it lying behind us and we steered directly for Dover.

The 25th of December - At daybreak we passed Romney Church, but before we could reach Dover, the wind became contrary, and we had to turn about until toward evening, when we began to tack.

The 26th of December - After the wind swung to our favor again last night, we were able to pass Dover this morning. Because the weather was rather bright, we could see the French coast. At twelve o'clock we dropped anchor at The Downs, near Deal. Our commodore and agent and six other ships, on which there were some of our troops, including the *Duke of Richmond,* had arrived here on the 23rd of the month. The names of those ships were *Elizabeth, Two Sisters, Hannah, Apollo, William,* and *Commerce.* On one ship, the Lengercke Grenadier Battalion had sailed from New York on 25 November, and on one, the Young Lossberg Regiment. Lieutenant [Georg] Schenck died the end of the month on the hospital ship *Jane,* and was buried at Carleton, in Ireland.

1784

The 3rd of January - After lying still, here at The Downs, since the 26th of last month, and after tolerating stormy weather during much of the time, we weighed anchor about noon and sailed for the Thames River. The weather was bright and pleasant, which made our voyage pleasant. We stayed close to the coast and could clearly see all the villages and estates on the coast. Lord Galland's estate stood out from all the rest, as regal. At eight o'clock in the evening, we dropped anchor near Margate.

The 4th - At daybreak we weighed anchor and took our course toward Sheerness, where we dropped anchor at twelve o'clock. At the mouth of the Thames more than 200 ships came toward us, which were bound in part to the East and West Indies, and to St. Augustine in Florida, and other regions. Rainy weather made the voyage unpleasant for us today.

The 5th of January - We lay still in the Medway River near Sheerness. We had pleasant spring weather, which, with a beautiful view of the surrounding islands, made today one of the most pleasant we have had since leaving New York. The large herds of cattle of every kind, grazing on the surrounding islands, gave the impression that this must be a very fertile region. The many grazing sheep are uncountable.

Here, in the river near Sheerness, lie a great many dismantled ships-of-the-line, and frigates. Sheerness is fairly secure, and has a ship-building yard, where very large ships-of-the-line are built. Two houses are built on old warships here, in which passengers coming from foreign lands are quarantined.

The 6th of January - At nightfall, we weighed anchor and sailed up the Medway River to Chatham, where we anchored between nine and ten o'clock in the evening. From Sheerness here, is sixteen English miles, in which distance, more than fifty dismantled ships-of-the-line and frigates lay. Considering their size, there are only twelve to thirty men on board [each] at present.

The 7th of January - We lay quietly at Chatham while quarters were arranged.

The 8th of January - We landed and entered the barracks. All our troops, from Major General von Wurmb, who commanded, on, were quartered in the barracks. The barracks are undoubtedly the best in the whole world. They are set on a hill, and surrounded by a wall which forms a quadrangle. There is a gate on each side of the quadrangle. The barracks for the officers are on a terrace, and face the barracks for the non-commissioned officers and privates. Outside the officers' barracks is a wide and beautiful walk along the top of a wall, which is planted with linden trees. In this barracks lie all the officers of the Linsing and Platte Grenadier Battalions, the Leib, Hereditary Prince, Prince Charles, and Young Lossberg Regiments, a detachment of the Donop Regiment, a part of the Artillery, and the hospital, and several English officers. Between the officers' and the privates' barracks is a large parade ground, to the west of which is the commandant's house, and to the east, the commodore's house. The barracks for the non-commissioned officers and privates are in three row buildings, one behind the other. In addition to those, which are built of stone and brick, there is one barracks behind, and located near the water, which is a barracks for land soldiers. It is also surrounded by a wall, and set apart from those barracks.

Near the barracks is a shipyard which is known to be one of the most important in England. Beside the ships-of-the-line presently being repaired herein, the ship *Leviathan,* 74 guns, is on the building blocks, and from all appearances will not be completed for some years. Fifteen hundred men from all professions are presently engaged continuously, working in this shipyard. The whole extensive shipyard, which is nearly an English mile long, is filled with all sorts of ship-building materials. No foreigner, not even an

Englishman, is allowed to see it without obtaining permission. We first had to get this permission from His Royal Majesty, who then allowed us to visit each week, on Tuesday and Friday. Non-commissioned officers and privates were not allowed in under any pretext.

Around the shipyard, the barracks, and the open town called Brompton, there are fortifications running from east to west, which, however, are not fully completed, and constitute a line of one and one-half English miles. These are occupied daily by two captains, four officers, and several hundred of our men.

The city of Chatham is a miserable place, and is not even worth notice. Rochester, adjoining Chatham, is more beautiful, and has an old and large cathedral, and a beautiful bridge over the Medway River, and by this means, Rochester and Stroat are connected. The entire surrounding area is hilly, but appears to be very fertile. Rochester sends two representatives to Parliament, and has a bishop.

<u>The 10th of January</u> - Lieutenant General Pitt arrived here and took command of the troops.

<u>The 18th of January</u> - The Queen's birthday was

celebrated, for which reason, toward noon, not only were all the cannons in the forts fired, but all the troops marched before the defenses, formed a line, and fired their small arms.

The 1st of April - As a result of the election of a new member to Parliament, which according to the English constitution, forbids any soldier being present at the voting place, all the English troops stationed here in the city and lying in the barracks had already marched to Maidstone eight miles from here, day before yesterday, and we had to embark today. Upon our arrival, we were not only welcomed here by the inhabitants in a polite manner, but also during our entire stay we were treated in the most friendly way, although the English soldiers had to vacate the barracks upon our arrival, and were then quartered in the inns of the city. The inhabitants would have gladly kept us with them longer, if they had had anything to say in the matter, even considering the inconveniences which they had been put to on our account. As a proof of our good discipline, I will note here an extract from the newspaper.

[In English]

Extract from St. James Chronicle from April 1th [sic] to April 3d 1784

The Hessian Troops are to embark on the 1th [sic] of April. Their Behavior during the Time they have been quartered here, has been sober and orderly. At public Worship they have shown a commendable Degree of Devotion and Attention. Too much cannot be said in Praise of the Civility and Politeness of the Officers, in short, they may, with justice, be proposed as Examples worthy the imitation of our Soldiery.

[Again in German]

The vote for the new member of Parliament took place today in Rochester, during the time when we were embarking, not far from the barracks.

The Platte Grenadier Battalion received two transport ships, the *Palliser*, on which were a part of those who came from America, and *Castor*. In addition to these two, the following ships belonged to the fleet: *Mary, Hannah, Betsy, Amphion, Everly, Saucy Ben, Myrtle, Charming Nancy,* and *Admiral Parker*, on which were Major General von Wurmb and the agent, Lieutenant Schaffcoth of the navy, *Mackeral, Fame,* and *Miriam.*

The 12th of April - As the wind was almost constantly contrary until today, we only sailed from Chatham today. The ship *Betsy*, due to a strong flood tide and a strong wind, ran against a warship and broke off the *Betsy's* aftermost mast, close to the deck, but caused no other damage. We anchored near Sheerness, where the ship *Neptune* joined us. Colonel von Wurmb was on board that ship, with a detachment of jaegers, who had been quartered in the barracks here.

The 14th of April - At daybreak the fleet, now numbering fifteen ships, departed in pleasant, beautiful weather. We sailed from Sheerness to the north along the English coast. About four o'clock in the afternoon our favorable wind swung to the east and forced us to enter the harbor at Harwich, where we anchored.

The 15th of April - We remained at Harwich.

The 16th of April - We had good, but very weak wind. At seven o'clock in the morning, we weighed anchor and set sail. Later the wind was somewhat stronger so that we passed Oxford, in Suffolk County, at twelve o'clock noon. With clear, bright weather, we had a pleasant voyage today. The nearby coast, covered with beautiful villages, cities, and estates, and the passing ships increased our pleasure. Toward evening we lost sight of the coast of England, which this evening caused our ship's company a certain amount of melancholy. "Who knows if we will see it again?" is often heard repeated.

The 17th of April - The weather and wind were the same as yesterday, and we could easily notice that we were living during springtime.

The 18th of April - At daybreak, the coast of The Netherlands could be seen from the top of the mast. According to our noon observation, we were at 53°20' north latitude. With a strong west wind, we sailed six English miles an hour. Several slow sailing ships, especially the *Neptune,* caused our progress to be greatly hindered today.

The 19th of April - Toward noon today we saw Helgoland, at the mouth of the Elbe River, to the northeast. Contrary wind, however, forced us to tack, and we had to pass the Weser River.

The 20th - Early this morning the wind veered to the west. It became very strong and drove us into the Weser. About one o'clock, we anchored near Bremerhaven. We encountered the ships which brought the Hessians from Portsmouth to Dover, here. The troops, however, had already disembarked and gone on the river to Bremen. After a short, happy, and pleasant voyage from England, we finally arrived, happily, back in Germany, after eight years. It must be conceded by everyone that we arrived here completely changed.

The 22nd of April - After being mustered, the Jaeger detachment, the Linsing Grenadier Battalion, and the detachment of the Donop Regiment, all of which arrived with us, were embarked on Bremen boats, and sailed for Bremen. A strong and contrary wind, however, made it necessary for this division to anchor near us.

The 26th of April - Although the debarkation of the Platte Grenadier Battalion and the Leib Regiment had been firmly set for the 24th of this month, because of a severe storm, which caused much damage in the area, and during which we saw three men from a Bremen boat drown near us, the landing was postponed until today. After being mustered, we left the English transport ship for the last time at noon today, and entered Bremen boats, which immediately set sail for Bremen on the rising flood tide.

The 28th of April - We arrived at Vegasack at noon. For the most part, the boats sailed alone, and each anchored where it pleased.

The 29th of April - This morning we reached

Bremen. We left the boats and embarked on Bremen barges. In Bremen, for the first time, the troops received bread which was made from crushed grain only, and very black. Upon receiving it, they made a very sour face and appeared much displeased with it. This was the first black, and furthermore, crushed grain bread which they had had in eight years. For the first time, they clearly understood that they were no longer in America, or England. We had five deserters here; the sixth was caught.

The 30th of April - We departed from Bremen and lay to for the night about a mile away. During the departure, two men of the Leib Regiment drowned close to the river bank.

The 5th of May - We arrived at Hoya, passing the bridge there, during the evening, in our barges, which took a long time.

The 6th of May - We spent the night near Nienburg. In the local armory, everything is in good order. Supposedly it contains weapons enough to arm 12,000 men.

The 10th of May - In the Prussian territories no non-commissioned officer or private was allowed ashore. The Prussians, however, worked to recruit our people. We met several good men from the Hessian regiments which preceded us, and who had been recruited at Minden.

The 11th of May - We stopped at Vlotho, the last place in Prussia, at noon, and the Prussian march commissary left us.

The 12th of May - We reached Rinteln. Twenty-three foreigners were given their discharges here, and they received a half-month's pay upon their departure.

The 13th of May - We left Rinteln.

The 14th of May - We passed Hameln, and remained overnight near the Grohnde city hall.

The 15th of May - We arrived at Polle.

The 16th of May - We passed Holzminden, where we halted at noon, and remained overnight a short distance this side of Hoexter.

The 17th of May - During the evening we arrived at Karlshafen.

The 18th of May - We sailed to Oedelsheim.

The 19th of May - We passed Veckerhagen, and remained lying at anchor overnight near a woods.

The 20th - Early this morning, at eight o'clock, we arrived at Hannover Muenden, where we remained on the 21st.

The 22nd of May - At six o'clock in the morning we left the barges, and began our march to Kassel on land. The baggage and artillery, which had been brought here yesterday, on other ships, was sent forward on the Fulda River. At eleven o'clock, the Platte Grenadier Battalion and the Leib Regiment marched onto the parade ground at Kassel. The latter remained in Kassel, and the first marched through the Castle Aue Gate, across the pontoon bridge to Sandershausen, where it was disbanded on the 23rd by Lieutenant General von Gohrs.

The 24th of May - The grenadier battalion disbanded and ceased to exist, and so this journal ends.

INDEX

THE AUTHOR

Bruce E. Burgoyne was born 25 October 1924 in Benton Harbor, Michigan, and is married with three grown sons. His wife Marie, a Doctor of Education from the University of Southern California, is a helpful research companion and source of encouragement. Mr. Burgoyne's education includes a Master of Arts in Social Science (History, Economics, and Government) from Trinity University in San Antonio, Texas, plus course work at half a dozen other colleges and universities in America and overseas. He has also completed numerous military courses in such subjects as German language, Counterintelligence, and Public Information.

His employment, in addition to recently teaching a seminar course on the Hessians at Delaware State University, has included twenty years of military service in the Navy, Army, and Air Force, and six years as a civilian intelligence officer with the Army. During his military and civilian service he lived six years in Germany during which time he attended German language school in Oberammergau and two months of in-depth study, living in German households and undergoing Berlitz-type training. His daily duties required interviewing and interrogating in German, which further developed his knowledge of the language.

His forty years of research on the role of the Hessians in the American Revolutionary War have taken him and his wife to archives in England and Holland, as well as those in Germany and the United States, and resulted in the translation of more than 35 major Hessian documents.

www.ingramcontent.com/pod-product-compliance
Lightning Source LLC
Chambersburg PA
CBHW071229170426
43191CB00032B/1166
9780788431579